Praise for *Finding the Wow*

"This is the perfect book if you're willing to ask yourself, 'Shall I take a chance and follow my dream?' And you want the answer to be 'Yes!' *Finding the Wow* is an inspiring story of courage to do what you love, and proof that it's never too late to reinvent the life you've always imagined."
— Maxine Clark, founder of Build-A-Bear Workshop at age 48

"If you've ever stuffed your dreams in a closet, read *Finding the Wow: How Dreams Take Flight at Midlife*. You will be inspired by this amazing story of how a determined mom soars to new heights and makes her dreams come true."
— Randy Peyser, author of *The Power of Miracle Thinking*

"Do you find yourself stuck in the routine of life? At midlife, MJ shares the craziness, hard work, setbacks, and glories of finding her wow. MJ's journey to live her wow will inspire you to find your own!"
— Laura Smith, airline pilot

finding
the
WOW

HOW DREAMS TAKE FLIGHT AT MIDLIFE

MJ Marggraff

ISBN: 978-0-9886191-9-7

Copyediting by Joanne Shwed, Author One Stop, Inc. (www.AuthorOneStop.com)

Interior design by Joanne Shwed, Backspace Ink (www.BackspaceInk.com)

Cover design by Kathi Dunn, www.dunn-design.com

Author photograph: LilyDongPhotography.com

Published in the United States by Big Table Publishing Company

Boston, MA
www.bigtablepublishing.com

www.MJMarggraff.com
mj@mjmarggraff.com

For Jim, Blake, and Annie ~
Your laughter gives each day wings.
With love.

And to an airplane named Bravo ~
We were born to meet.

Whatever your airplane is ~ fly it.

"When once you have tasted flight, you will forever walk
the earth with your eyes turned skyward,
for there you have been,
and there you will always long to return."
~ Leonardo da Vinci

Finding the Wow

How a Pilot Got Her Start

YOU WOULDN'T THINK that losing a weekly planning book would be such a big deal; that it has the power to knock you off your feet, force you to look at what's really going on in your life, and make you see yourself in a completely new way. But that's what is happening to me.

This spring morning starts like most mornings, with the alarm's buzz demanding me to begin another day. I groan and punch it quiet but, instead of dozing, I obsess about the day's duties. After a few minutes, I get up and head downstairs.

As usual, I reach for it even before I make coffee. But my hand just sort of hovers above empty space where the planner usually lay. Not there? Wait. What? So strange not to see it that I actually need a few seconds to process the fact that it's not there.

Where the hell …? What day is it? Maybe Saturday? No, a school day. What am I supposed to do on—whatever day this is? A committee meeting or the field trip? What do my children do after school? Am I meeting with a teacher?

Panicking, I try to remember where I'd last seen it.

Breathe. You'll find it. But so many others rely on my planner. I can't let anyone down. What did I promise today? Calm down. You'll find it, and everything will go back to normal.

Normal. In other words, a jam-packed schedule of things that have to be done. Still staring at the spot on the counter where the planner should be, I realize that without it my basic identity is missing too. How did an $8 appointment book become the blueprint to my life?

I dart around, searching everywhere, until it is time to wake Jim and the kids. Distractedly, I make breakfast for everyone and try to participate in the morning chitchat. Inside is chaos. I feel like a passenger left behind at the station while the train with all my instructions pulls out.

I'd left corporate life almost five years earlier because I wanted to be at home with our kids Blake and Annie after we moved from New England to California. On many days the challenges of parenthood rival those of my professional years—minus the paycheck and enticing stock options. Sure, I miss the camaraderie of my colleagues, but as a mom I have new friends: I belong to the legions of parents who share the motto, "We Serve"—in boardrooms, classrooms, and charities, and daily in the kitchen. The days are long, and every moment is spoken for.

"You okay?" Jim asks.

"I lost my planner."

He butters his toast. "I'm sure it'll turn up."

Easy for him to say. He is a stable, sane person. As I sip coffee and watch my family, it occurs to me that even worse than not having all my assignments laid out for me is the disappearance of my reward system. I love accomplishing tasks and, when I cross out each one, it's like my planner is saying, "Another thing done! Great job!"

As soon as everyone is done eating, Jim retreats to his office upstairs, and I get the kids off to school. When I resume my search, it is with considerably less enthusiasm. I know that when I find the planner, my life will go back to the way it was.

And I am not sure that is what I want.

Planners keep our focus on what's ahead but can also be a grim reminder of time passing. Middle age is upon me, and suddenly I know with powerful certainty that I do *not* want to look back on my life and find nothing but funny motherhood anecdotes. I don't want to regret passing up dreams that go unfulfilled because I'd again agreed to bake 60 cupcakes, build a cardboard castle, sell raffle tickets, or dress up as a large gift box in order to sell wrapping paper for Annie's class fund-raising project.

I've filled 40 planners with tasks related to school, college, work, marriage, children, building, moving ... how thrilling it would be to have a new planner of pages filled with fun things; things that would reconnect me to my dream! At once my inner voice pipes up: *It's a bit late. I bet you don't even remember what your dream is.*

Oh, but I do. I do.

Okay, fine. So you remember. But come on. Learn to fly an airplane? You're in your 40s. You've got children to take care of! This is a time to be grounded. Find another dream.

When had this happened to me? When had I become addicted to being busy? Why did all the other moms seem so content?

"I want more," I hear myself say in a whiny voice. Then I feel guilty. It is wrong to be unhappy.

Quit complaining. Find the planner, and let's get back on track.

But I stop looking. I pour another cup of coffee, and I sit at the kitchen table, and I look at my life.

Stop this. Go out and buy another planner. Come on.

I've wanted to learn to fly ever since I was a little girl; I never wanted to be a ballerina or a movie star like my friends did. So what happened? Being sensible. Education, career, husband, children.

I stand, head back upstairs, tell Jim I am going out, and drive to the stationery store. Holding my new daily planner for the year 2003, I sigh at the blank pages. A fresh canvas. How to fill the pages was up to me: Same life ... or a new life?

Reflection

"NOT NOW!" I SHOUT at all the other drivers, each with their needle stuck on the speed limit. Everyone in the world is in front of me on this highway.

"Moron!"

I'm finally able to pass someone who should know better than to be in the left lane. Our eyes meet, and she gives me a sweet smile instead of the angry finger I deserve. If the police pull me over, I'll tell them I'm on my way to the ER.

An ambulance, red lights spinning and siren wailing, carefully threads its way between lanes. *Great, now we're all stopped.* As it passes me, I try not to look—that could be her.

"Josephine is on her way to the hospital," said the caller earlier. "We found her on the floor." *Again,* they could have added. Her ailments keep coming, her hospital visits too frequent.

After my parents died many decades ago, my father's older sister Aunt Jo took me under her wing. I was still somebody's child as long as I had her. At barely 5 feet tall, she has been a source of wisdom wrapped up with a great sense of humor, and I'm the daughter she never had.

"Sorry, but you'll have to go solo on this one," Jim had said. "I won't be home in time."

Right now, alone is not a good situation for me. The traffic creeps. I'm miserable and scared and irrationally angry. She'd better not be thinking about checking out. She's only 90! Isn't that the new 80? Surely there must be a decade or two left in her. She must know how unfinished I am. How unready for a life without her. My tears become another driving hazard.

A million memories are in the car with me: Aunt Jo in the kitchen, stirring a pot on the stove, dressed in an oversized apron, helping me clarify the perplexities of youth; examining the cause and effect on an array of subjects like jealousy, love letters, the death of my dog, competition among friends, my delayed physical development, Buddhism, and math anxiety, while punctuating the important points of each with her wooden stirring spoon.

"Taking time to understand is hard work," she'd said many times, "but paying attention to it is its own reward." Her best line was about true love: "Do 'it' swinging from the chandeliers if it pleases the two of you!"

When I first heard this counsel at 14, I was unsure of the mechanics of love and even less certain of its metaphors—besides, we didn't have a chandelier. As I eased into adulthood, I came to appreciate her as a trustworthy source of knowledge on the mysteries of life; a confidential ally who could read me better than anyone, even Jim.

Blast-blast! The horn from the car behind wakes me from a haze of reminiscing. The traffic is again moving, slowly.

"Okay, okay!" I say as I rejoin the present. "What's your hurry?"

Jogging into the now familiar ER, I ask the woman at the desk if Josephine Warnken has come in.

"Older woman wearing a white wig?"

"Yes, that would be her."

"She just got here. Come this way."

As I follow her, I try not to make eye contact with patients lying on gurneys in rooms with curtains only half closed. The place hasn't changed much since I was here long ago for my parents, its atmosphere still stale with sadness.

Beep beep beep beep comes the monotonous notes from the monitors—the counting machines, measuring, announcing the finite number of heartbeats for this one, breaths for that one.

18

"Here she is," announces my escort. "Someone will be in to talk to you soon."

"Thanks."

I hurry to Aunt Jo's side. She's wearing her wig, which seems like a very good sign. A permanent fixture atop her head for as long as I can remember, it's a full, silvery-white-looking thing that no one at any age would be naturally endowed with, but it is the fashion accessory that she never leaves home without. She's asleep, so I sit in an uncomfortable plastic chair and shut my eyes. *Please be okay. Please be okay. Please, please, please.*

"Why are you crying?" Aunt Jo asks softly. She slips her hand from under the blankets and takes mine, moving her head carefully to regard me with her tired, blue eyes.

"I heard you were here." I clear my throat and continue, "... and thought I might come by to take you out to lunch."

She blinks with a small smile.

"Let's get you out of here," I whisper, biting my bottom lip to stop any more glib remarks.

"Listen," she says, and I wait to hear her scold me about crying or leaving other, more important things to come see her. "I've heard how they let you out," she finishes with a cough.

I'm not sure yet if what she's going to tell are the meds talking, but with her it might be a well-laid scheme. "What's your plan?"

"They will ask questions. I will answer perfectly. Then they'll let me go. First, they'll ask me my name."

"Answer 'Methuselah,'" I joke hopefully.

She coughs a few times, takes a moment to gather up her energy, and goes on. "Then, address and phone number. Help me review this so I get it right, Mary."

I dig in my pocket for a tissue, daring to hope she'll have another chance.

"They may even ask me for my political party."

I say, "Answer 'Republican,'" and wait to see if she has any of her humor. I need a laugh right away or I will surrender to uncontrollable tears.

Please play with me, Aunt Jo, I hear myself at six say in that wheedling tone children have.

"Idiot," she finally almost grins but is taken over by another fitful, congested cough attack.

"Is that your party of preference or just a pet name for me?" I'd love to see her smile, but she can't. Neither can I. She drifts away into hazy sleep, my matriarch under a silver-wig cloud.

A nurse pops her head in and gestures for me to come out; the doctor is available. The facts are that health complications prevent my aunt's valiant attempt to escape from the hospital. Nor will she dodge the illnesses and recent injury that have claimed her good humor.

"There are options to prolong her life. Say, for some days or weeks. But not cure her. She is wearing out," the doctor says as he hands me more tissues. "It's your call."

I am so thankful that he just stands there to let me say how difficult it is to hear him explain it, as expected as his news is. They get our pain, I realize. How do they do this for a living, the staff and doctors, dealing with the end, day after day? I never could.

It's your call. It's not though, not really. Aunt Jo already made her philosophy clear, and I will respect it: "Existing is not living." The doctor has just told me that this is the end of her run.

I return to the bed where her small body barely makes a mound under the blanket and silently take my seat again. There's a sense of finality in the air.

After several minutes of silence, unsure if she's aware of me sitting there, if she can talk, or if she even wants to, I ask, "Want to practice your answers?"

"What?" she says, opening her eyes, sighing deeply, and coughing. "No. Let's talk about you."

"Me? Why?"

She looks my way. "You have more—tomorrows."

"It's you I want. To see you tomorrow."

"I love you." Her chest rattles. "Dreams …"

20

I wait, and when she doesn't go on, I ask, "What do you mean? You're having bad dreams?"

"Big dreams. It's why" ... another coughing fit ... "we're here."

She's coughing so hard now that I grab the remote and press the button to get a nurse in.

"Don't try to talk," I say.

"Dream big. You ... need to ... you need to do this."

The nurse hurries in with a paper cup that has a pill in it. "Something for the cough," she explains. I stand and step out of the way and watch while she gives Aunt Jo the pill and coaxes her to take a sip of water. "It'll probably knock her out."

In other words, my Aunt Jo is too sick to even be awake. I feel sick, dizzy, and scared but somehow numb all over. I sit and find her hand.

"Mary," Aunt Jo says in a voice that's so weak I can hardly hear her, "don't be afraid."

Does she mean don't be afraid of losing her ... or of following big dreams?

"I won't," I promise.

"Work like mad," she says, but already she's drifting out. Is she delirious?

"I will," I assure her.

"She'll probably be out for a while," the nurse says again, "if you want to go get coffee or something to eat or something."

"No, I want to stay."

"Okay. I'll check back in a bit."

"Thank you."

I nod, and she bustles out; places to go, people to save.

For a few seconds I stroke Aunt Jo's hand, her skin thin as tissue paper. I want to ask her what she means about dreams and not being afraid, but she's asleep, and what pours out instead is a torrent of memories: stories of my favorite times with her as well as some confessions, like how I caught skipper-jacks on her marigolds when I was three and thought I was doing them a favor by wiping the gold dust from their wings, then was crushed to learn they needed it to live.

21

I dig deeper to uncover thoughts put away so long ago and so painful to open: her stories of losing her children and how I wish I'd had them as cousins; how she knew that my dad was hard to please but easy to infuriate, and how I'd run to her and Uncle Chris so I could be told I was not so bad; that I learned how to be a loving mom because of her.

Later, as the world outside slips into indigo, the nurse brings me a pillow and blanket. I rest my head on the end of the bed.

Someone moves me. "Wake up, honey. Sit up."

I lift my head, neck stiff. "What? Aunt Jo?"

But it wasn't Aunt Jo. It was the nurse. "I'm sorry, honey. She's gone."

I drive to her small, ranch-style house, where roses grow in neat rows, to sort through her belongings and souvenirs of life. It's up to me to choose what to keep and cherish, and what to let go of to become someone else's treasure.

In her closet, an unexpected stockpile of wigs: all the same shape, synthetic sheen, and color. At least 20 of them, many on faceless, white, styrofoam heads. I grab my phone to call Jim and tell him.

"Closets," he says. "They hold the genies of our stories. Can I have the heads?"

I say yes without even asking why. We hang up, and I keep going.

I find the diary she kept when she was dating my uncle and learn that he was a fantastic kisser: *And How!* My father though, her then six-year-old little brother, was a regular menace, spying but reporting to his sister when their dad was near. But to leave the young lovers alone, he'd been easily bought off with a nickel to spend at the candy store. Soon after, my aunt discovered that he'd been a double agent, compensated as well by their father for his reports. I can't help laughing; how often I'd heard him say he'd been a perfect child. I put the diaries into a box marked "SAVE." These diaries will be my most cherished keepsakes.

Boxes of sheet music fill several shelves. Among them, the traditional English Christmas music, "The Holly and the Ivy." I still can hear echoing from years far away, when I was a little girl at their small house on

Christmas night. We played and sang together, decorated in greens and reds, with the fireplace snapping its own tune.

A couple of years ago, when my son Blake was seven, he played the same tune on the piano at a holiday recital. Of course, Aunt Jo was there and loved it, her hands clasped to her chest. (I first worried it was a heart attack.)

"Wonderful!" she'd exclaimed. "I couldn't have played it better myself."

Blake beamed.

It was last Christmas when our daughter Annie, two years younger than her brother, played her new clarinet for Aunt Jo; her last Christmas, it turned out. The tunes sounded familiar, she said to Annie, but the titles escaped her.

And then come the books. The ones that lasted through the years have been reduced to a sparse few. My aunt and uncle were part of an international fraternal order of similar-minded folks, who believed we have the capacity to create a positive world order and can find personal happiness—ideas that confounded other family members, who whispered behind closed doors about the oddness of such notions.

Volumes on world history, religions, or esoteric cosmic consciousness have long been donated to special libraries, except for one I'd bought for my uncle on my first trip abroad, in a London bookstore tucked in the shadows along a narrow street. My uncle had written the name of the bookstore and its address on a scrap of paper and had asked me to see if a particular title might be available. I made sure to execute this errand and get it for him, to thank him for buying my airplane ticket. After several hours of touring musty, dark-paneled shops housing esoteric books, I found what he wanted: *The Infinite Power: Secrets of Ancient Cultures and the Powers of the Modern Mind*.

The old proprietor behind the desk scowled, his big hands slowly rubbing the leather cover as if it were overdue for the affection it deserved. "How do you know this subject?" he snapped.

"I ... I don't," I answered, startled. "It's for my uncle who travels and speaks on the topic. He's a recognized expert in ancient symbols and rituals. He'll read it—gratefully."

The bookseller examined me sternly, as if trying to decide if I were worthy of purchasing the book. Then he muttered, "Right," slipped it into a bag, and accepted my money.

Now it has come back to me. Like the old man, probably long gone, I rub the leather cover. I open it to the page with my thank-you-note bookmark and find a poem written in his handwriting:

The Dragon's Teeth

The dragon,
Ready, ravenous, and in you resides
To feast on your cherished dreams inside.

Yesterday's imaginings instead
Have been replaced with doubt, fear, and dread.

This force of terror will tip the scales;
As your life reduces, it prevails.

With that, the dragon, as fear, devours
Life from life through the years and hours.
How does your dream design a shield?
Or must all beloved passions yield?

The dragon's fight will not be finished
But yours to face, yours to diminish.

Your armor—knowledge—opens the skies
Forging paths of courage to conquer lies.

Triumphant, twice, will the story,
When you slay your dragon and live
your glory.

At the bottom he had written in red ink, "*REMEMBER THIS!*" I touch his penmanship to reach out across the years and be closer to him again. Then I put the poem back into the book and set it aside, the wise advice to be considered later.

Keep going, I think through tears. *Get through this.*

On to the really scary stuff, which might be enough to open a voodoo shop. Aunt Jo and Uncle Chris traveled to exotic lands, met statesmen of countries, spoke several languages, and had acquired many mementoes: masks, large and small, of animals and creatures of residences unknown, used to line the walls of my uncle's study, and one particularly creepy one always made me run from the room when I was little. My uncle said that people from primitive tribes made masks to keep bad spirits away. As I look through them, the only thing that scares me is how fast Jim would want to keep them—more, even, than the styrofoam heads. I pack them all in a few boxes marked "DONATE."

For a few minutes I sit on the floor, surrounded by all of these things, and think, *This is what they did for excitement, how they filled the daily planners of their lives.* And I never felt emptier inside.

Annie loves ballet classes—she jumps and spins, wearing pink netting over pink leotards and stockings that bag at the knees. Blake takes tae kwon do, where arms and legs blast into different trajectories. I sit in the back of their classes and witness a pink, whirling dervish, who rises when all other little dervishes go down, or a boy encased in stiff, white cotton, out of which hands and feet strike the air in all directions.

Inspired to add some zest to our busy schedules, I signed up Jim and me for tango classes. Together we slide and lunge about the floor, like bumper cars colliding to a Latin beat, but I suppose it's only a matter of time before I admit that I don't like it, and we stop going. I'm not a kid engaged in life's dance; I'm a grown-up, and trying to have fun is hard work when my heart's not in it.

I heft a tower of folded laundry and head into our room. On the floor and around the bed are piles of books; a lover of reading a lot of different things at a time, Jim uses anything he can find to keep his place—pens, envelopes, even socks.

He looks up as I come in. "What exciting things will you do today?" he asks innocently.

Standing there, holding my mountain of laundry, I can't even answer. He invents talking books and globes, and his creativity is prolific. Each day new ideas are born in his office in the next room—nests of wires loop wildly around walls and tables where drafts of words and pictures zap into electric life, and faint sounds of whistling voices coming to life rise and fall. A modern-day Dr. Frankenstein's lab.

What exciting things will I do today? I only have the energy to shrug.

At Aunt Jo's house there is still a lot to go through, and as I empty drawers and fill boxes, I think about the day Blake and Annie will be doing this with my stuff. I picture them finding a huge box on the highest shelf of the closet, and on it the word "IMPORTANT." I picture them peering inside and seeing not photos, letters, and treasured keepsakes but all of my appointment calendars.

I picture their disappointment. I picture Annie, shaking her head and saying, "*Why*, Mom?"

I think about Aunt Jo's words about dreams. I think about the dragon poem. I pull out my phone.

"Hi, Helen," I say when she answers, then my words cascade out: "I'd like to get together. I need to talk. I'm having … I'm feeling like … when can we get together?"

I hear the rustle of pages. "Let's see," she says. "You and Joan and I have our book club on Monday."

"Perfect. But let's not talk about the book. Let's talk about us."

"Us?"

"What we're doing. What we're not doing. What we can do to make our lives more meaningful."

She hesitates a long time, then moans softly. I know without being able to see her that she's scowling and worried that I'm adding something to her busy month's page. It's exactly what I would do if someone hit me with this desperate kind of phone call. Like me, she's a serial volunteer. Agrees to every request, then feels resentful about how much she does. Signs up for more, feels more resentment. Still, she's energetic and gives good advice. I've known her for several years through our children.

"We're overdue for this, Helen. You. Me. Joan. What do you say?"

"I'm not sure what you're asking me, MJ. I don't have time to do another thing ... really, I don't. With a school election coming up, I'm flat out right now. And lately I've been so tired. It's all I can do to get everyone through supper, and then I'm ready for bed."

"I don't mean volunteering to do something. Of course you're tired of that. I want to really look at how we all spend our time, with whom or what, and how to look at life—with excitement." It sinks in belatedly, what she said about the election. "Don't tell me you're running again! I'm not going to vote for you. I don't want you to win."

Another long pause, then she says, "So we'll be meeting on our book club night, right? But instead of talking about books, we're going to talk about what we're doing ... what we should be doing ..."

I can tell she's actually writing it down. This is what we've been reduced to—her, me, and my other midlife friends. I picture us all in our 80s, sitting up in bed, reaching for our appointment calendars, and writing in our scratchy, old-lady writing, "Get up ... put on robe ... take pills ... eat breakfast ... breathe."

"Can you call Joan and let her know?"

"What exactly should I tell her?"

"That we are going to talk about dreams. And dragons."

Silence, and then I hear her murmur, "Dreams and ... what?"

The Chicks in Charge

"SO WAIT. LET ME SEE if I understand this," Joan says. She and Helen have been sitting quietly for several minutes, listening to me try to explain. "You're looking to change your routine. You want to start something new. And, out of *all* the things to do, you choose learning to fly ... an *airplane*?"

I nod.

"That's a little crazy. No, wait. That's a *lot* crazy." She looks at Helen. "Don't you think so?"

"Joan," Helen says, "if you don't have something nice to say, don't say anything. Didn't your mother ever teach you that?"

"You don't have to be nice," I say. "Be honest. Because, honestly, I think maybe I *am* going crazy."

"Not crazy," Helen says promptly.

"I'm 45. My parents are gone. The people who raised me are gone. Life is short. I want to know when it's my turn; that I touched the stars I wanted to touch."

They're silent, impressed by my speech. I'd come up with the line about touching the stars last night and am pleased it seems to have struck a chord. Or maybe they're just startled.

Then Joan asks, "Have you talked to Jim about it yet?"

"Not yet."

"Flying is so dangerous. Why not come up with another dream? One that—no offense—makes sense." She holds up one of my fresh-from-the-oven cinnamon buns. "Like these. All you had to do was take them out of the fridge, break open the package, and bake them. But they're sort of burned, a little. You could take some baking lessons."

"Me in the kitchen is dangerous," I say. I'm not offended by her criticism—I'd put the buns in and then got distracted. When the buzzer went off, I kept looking up flight schools in the phone book for five more bottom-burning minutes. "Next time bring yours," I say; her buns are legendary.

Joan puts it back on the plate. "I'm just saying that, if I announced something like that to Roger, he'd burst out laughing. Then he'd call all of his friends, and they'd laugh too."

"I'm not going to give up my dream just because my husband might laugh at it." Feeling a little sorry for the mostly blackened cinnamon buns, I pick one up and defiantly take a bite, chew, and swallow, and then have a hasty gulp of coffee to wash it down. "When I was a little girl, all my friends dreamed of getting married. A few of them wanted to be secretaries. And then get married. Know what I wanted to be? An astronaut. I knew none of the other girls wanted that. I sneaked out books from the library so I wouldn't be teased. Well ..." I pick up my cinnamon bun, change my mind, and put it back down. "... I missed out on being an astronaut. But a pilot— that could, maybe, still happen. No, I wouldn't be your typical student pilot. But should I accept that again—that it's different from the other moms— and give up?"

"Absolutely not!" Helen's sharp response takes us by surprise. "Look." She digs out her planner from her purse and holds it up, flipping through the pages so that we can see that almost every date has something written on it. "Sometimes I look at this thing, and I wonder how the hell it all happened! I'm like you, MJ—I never dreamed of being a wife and a mother. I wanted to work for a big company, make a lot of money, and go on business trips. The corporate life. That's what I wanted. And that's what I had too." She puts the planner back in her purse. "All I do is volunteer now. Literally, it's *all I do*."

We're a little shocked; we thought she loved volunteering.

"Maybe it's a midlife crisis, or whatever you want to call it," she goes on, "but I'd love to feel passion again. About something."

30

"I like routine," Joan declares. "I'm sorry, but I do. I like being a wife. I like knowing what I'm going to be doing every day. I don't like surprises."

"Well, that's valid," I say.

"The thing is, I've been out of the workforce for so long that I wouldn't even know what I wanted to do. I have a good life. Roger has given me *a good life*." She reaches into her purse and pulls out her planner. "Let's see. Monday nails, then go to Nordstrom's ..."

It doesn't feel right to remind her about all the times she's told us she can't stand Roger and wants to leave him. Are they getting along better? Or has she just gone numb?

"Besides," she goes on, "what if Jim doesn't want you to learn to fly? You've got two kids. What if he thinks it's too dangerous? What if he just says no? It's not worth risking your marriage. Is it?"

Helen flips her hand dismissively. "He'll be fine with it."

"What if he's not? What if he says no?" Joan persists. "What will you do? And you have to think of the kids. Of the marriage. You've got to be reasonable."

"I ..."

"What if Jim thinks you need this because he and the kids aren't enough? What if the kids don't want you to do it? What if they're too scared that you'll ... that something will happen to you? What will you say to them when they come to you crying because they're scared?"

"That's something MJ needs to find out," says Helen, just as we're interrupted by the ringing of a cell phone. We all check to see who will claim ownership.

"Mine," sighs Helen, flipping it open. "Hi. What's the matter? Well, okay, we'll talk about it later ... Because I'm in a meeting. Love you. Bye ... What?" She looks at us and shakes her head. "Yes, of course it's an *important* meeting. All my meetings are." She punches off. "My children think meetings are a waste of time."

Another phone chirps—Joan's. "You need what? When? Tell me what it look like." Her shoulders fall. "You looked on your desk? Under the stack of ... okay, I'll look for it when I get home. Bye." She snaps her phone shut. "It would take an archeologist to find anything under the pile of crap on his desk." She shakes her head. "I may not have children, but I do have one big kid."

The room falls silent. I feel my eyes go to the scarf tied around Joan's head.

"A bad dye job," she'd explained when she came in. She'd also told us that her fingers hurt; she'd gotten an infection from a manicure and was on antibiotics. Despite our reassurance that she's beautiful, she doesn't see it; she's not hearing it from Roger, and our praise means nothing.

I hold back a shudder. I would hate to have my entire self-esteem resting on the shoulders of an unappreciative husband.

"Anyway," I say, "is it too much to ask to feel energized? Tantalized? Absorbed by something intriguing? Years ago my uncle told me ... I asked him what real love is; I was about 20 ... and he said that love will run you dry and fill you up at the same time. That passions come with exhilaration and exhaustion. Build you up and wear you out." (I keep the rest of what he said to myself because it feels too big for the room: "The mountain will not be easy, Mary. But the view, glorious.") "He said life is all about finding your wow."

"Finding your wow," Helen repeats softly. "I love that. I think you're really on to something here. It's a you-know-it-when-you-feel-it thing. I can't say for sure what *it* is. For me. But it's definitely different from what I've been doing. Day after day after day. I'm not happy. So I ... that is, I've been ... doing something different."

"Go on," I say when she pauses.

"I bought a camera and a book on photography a few months ago. While the kids are at school, I go out to my garden and take pictures."

"Of what?"

"Of all the little worlds in the world out there. Things most people wouldn't see. Morning sun on a birdhouse. Moss on the gate's hinge. Rust on a nail that ivy winds around. Small things that feel powerful to me."

"That's fantastic! What do Brad and the kids say about this?"

"I haven't told them. Or anyone. Until now."

"But Helen, what's the point in keeping it to yourself?" Joan asks. "If you love it so much ... it's not like you're doing anything wrong."

32

"I know. It just feels weird to be doing something, you know, for *me*. And someday … well, my dream is to someday have my own exhibit, and even sell them."

"You just one day decided you wanted to take photographs?" Joan inquired.

"No, no. Like MJ, I've had this dream my whole life. Since I got one of those Kodak Instamatic cameras. I was just a kid."

"Proof," I say, "that dreams never die. When can we see some of your pictures?"

"Soon. Not quite yet."

"I'm trying to remember what my childhood dreams were," Joan says.

"I read somewhere that it's what we still long for. Somewhere in the attics of our hearts," I say. "So can we all think about what we might have left in that attic? Then meet again? I need a sounding board. Whether I dare go on or stay grounded; break rules or follow them. If all my ideas go up in smoke and not up in the air, I need your support—and challenge. And, if nothing else, you can tell me if I'm nuts or not."

"You're nuts," says Joan, but she's smiling.

I smile back. "Let's commit to each other to take charge of our lives."

"And our planners!" Helen adds.

"And our dreams, whatever they are," I say. "Let's find out what else can be written inside a planner with a year's worth of pages."

"I haven't felt that way in a long time," Helen says. "In charge."

"The Chicks in Charge," I say.

"I'm in. Joan?"

Joan rolls her eyes but says, "Sure."

"Jim? Are you awake?" No response. Steady breathing. Snoring. Asleep. *Forget it.*

I roll over to try to sleep too, lying as still as I can while the night takes me away; my head swimming in memories. Trying to remember.

Semi-drowsing I watch a fog lift from the bedroom I had when I was six: green-dotted Swiss drapes that I loved because my grandmother made them and an artwork montage of crayon drawings. Books on the floor, open to pictures of flight and space and stars—the mysteries I loved to read about. In the corner, an Easy-Bake oven—a birthday gift of such devastating disappointment that I cried, but one that became a favorite when I turned it into a spaceship with my stuffed bears recruited as the astronauts. A rocket I made on the shelf, and a few wooden airplane models. Space, stars, air, and clouds whirl …

My vision continues, years go by, and the world rushes past. I can hear it hum, like the small planes I rode in when I was in college but couldn't afford the lessons. To have my own skies. My own wings. So real that I feel the wind.

Sinking into sleep, I am solo but not totally alone. Something else is there. But before I can see who or what, I am falling. I catch myself in time and shake myself awake. Relieved to feel my bed. And hear gentle snoring again.

"Jim." How can someone sleep so soundly? "Jim!"

Snoring sputters, slows, then stops. "What? What is it?"

"Sorry. Did I wake you?"

"Yeah." He yawns and readjusts his position, back to me now.

I put a finger between his shoulder blades and make a little circle. "Jiiimmm …"

"Oh, hon, that's nice, but I can't tonight. Have an early morning. Tomorrow though."

"No, I want to talk to you about something."

He groans; like most men, finds "talk" a more appealing activity during the day. "About the children?"

"No."

He stretches, one long breath expelled. "*Ooookaaay.* Awake now. So?"

"I've been thinking."

"Uh oh."

"Listen. Seriously. I'd like to … I want to … go back to school."

"Sounds like a great idea."

So far so good. "It's sort of like, not really a regular course."

"Is it something we can talk about tomorrow?"

"No."

He waits, and when I don't embellish, says, "*What.*"

"Yeah, okay." I say, very fast, "I want to learn to fly."

In the darkness I feel him staring. "You want to learn to fly. A plane?"

No, my old Easy-Bake oven. "Yes, a plane."

"Oh."

"You've heard me talk about it over the years. How I always wanted to."

"Well, I mean, yeah, but you haven't talked about it in a long time. Since we had the kids, I don't think."

I can't tell from his tone how he feels about it. "But I still want to do it."

"Learn to fly."

"An airplane. Yes."

"Do you ... I mean, it's kind of ..." he sits up. "Do you think you want this because you want a change from the routine of being at home? Is that it? Maybe we should get away for a while, just the two of us. We could leave Blake and Annie with neighbors ..."

"No," I say. "I mean, that does sound great. But if we did that, when we came home, I would still want to do this."

He reaches out and touches my shoulder. "Now, don't take this the wrong way ..."

I bristle.

"But maybe this is how it starts."

"Maybe this is how *what* starts?"

"Menopause. The need for a change is really, you know, *the change* happening ..."

"It is *not* menopause," I say, holding back anger. "It's not some spur-of-the moment idea. I need to try this and want you to be behind me." I flop back on my pillow. "*Menopause.*"

Long silence. I hear crickets in the yard and a bird chirping; awake this late? I picture the male, sleeping in the nest, and the female nudging him, wanting to talk: "We need a new nest. I need to spread my wings." Come morning they will both wake and take to the skies ... my dream. *Ironic, isn't it?* My thoughts are getting fuzzy.

35

"I need to think about it," Jim says finally. He lies back down.

I open my mouth but know not to push. Not like I expected him to say, "Oh, my God, yes! This is *exactly* what you should do!"

I lie back down too. "Sorry I woke you," my voice a tiny bit sullen.

"It might be … okay," he says.

"What? Really?"

"*Might* be."

I sit up again. "This is great! Listen, I have a plan. A plan to work it all in. What I can do is—"

"MJ, I can't think right now. I need to sleep. We can talk tomorrow. But one thing is not up for debate."

"What?"

"No helicopters. Just airplanes."

"Sure. Sure. Of course." I should leave it alone. I should … "But, just so I know, why not?"

"Too dangerous. You have to be a mother first, pilot second."

"Of course," I say. I punch the air in silent victory.

He drifts off, but I lie awake until light creeps through the window.

The alarm goes off, jarring me awake. Hammering it with my fist to make it stop, everything's blurry. What happened last night? Trying to remember the exact words. But no time now. Must get up and get to the elementary school and to a parents' club meeting.

Jim's already gone, and I see a note that he's left on his pillow: "No helicopters."

I brighten and quickly throw off the blankets.

"I'd like to get this meeting started!" Helen announces to a room full of energetic parents' club moms and a few dads.

"Hey, Helen. Can I add something to the agenda? It's not a big deal, just a quick request. It would be a big help to me and my committee," asks a mom of a first-grader.

"Sure, but just a few minutes. We have a long morning ahead."

The chatter in the room echoes off the walls. I know this room too well: how the linoleum sounds under my shoes when I walk in; how there are always crumbs on the tables from the snacks of the young students. I look at the clock, with its no-nonsense big face, and the minute hand that moves with a *click* each time 60 seconds passes. *How many kids have learned to tell time on that clock? How many of us now let time tell us what to do?*

"Is this the meeting when we finalize the room parties?" asks another parent. "If it is, I'll stay. But if not, I have a TON of things I have to do …"

I sit back, sigh. We'll be here until lunchtime!

"I'd like to open the floor for discussion on where the money from our fund-raiser should be spent," Helen leads. She is beautiful, dressed in jeans; white oxford shirt; and a crisp, maroon-colored jacket. Hands instantly go up, and Helen calls on each by name.

As the ideas come in earnest, I fade out to review my plan: From here I should be able to get to the airfield—the small one in Concord—in 30 minutes, and talk to someone about enrolling in flight classes. I will study in the evenings, after the children have gone to bed. There are a couple of committees I can trim from my planner.

"Should we talk about what happened last time, when we ran out of milk and some of the children had to drink water?"

I look out the window. *What will it be like to move through the skies?* I try to picture it: racing down a runway, pulsing with speed like trembling violins, then rise on wings lifted higher by a tenor of wind, and at the first turn all the horns join in, lifting, lifting …

"MJ!"

"Yes!" Startled, I look up, then down at the agenda. I have no idea what we're talking about. "What?"

"The ballot. I need your votes in. Now."

"Oh. Right." I have no idea what the vote is about.

"Moving on to the next item …"

I can't stay. I just can't. I collect my papers and stuff them into my folders.

"Excuse me," I say to the other parents as I pass behind their chairs and go up to Helen. "Helen," I whisper as the others are again immersed in lively discussions. "I'm going to the airfield."

She looks at me, then breaks into a smile. "Good for you. Call me later?"

"I will."

As I walk out the door I hear her say: "MJ has to leave for an appointment. Next item ..."

I drive to the airfield, pull up to the buildings, and for a long time just sit in the car. Now that I'm here, my dream doesn't seem exciting and magical; it seems really, really scary. I picture my airplane going down ... the needle on *empty* while lightning flashes and torrential rain makes visibility impossible. Impact is inevitable. My children growing up without me. Will Jim blame me?

Stop this. You've wanted to do this your whole life. You'll hate yourself if you chicken out. You will regret it forever.

I shut off the engine, climb out of the car slowly, and slink inside. No one is around. There are brochures on the counter. I grab one and run out.

From the Ground Up

THE COFFEE SHOP is infused with an aroma of dark roast so deep that you can taste it before it's in your cup. My attention drifts from my book to the view out the window: skies of blue, veiled in vapor-thin clouds; hills sporting early fall colors of butterscotch grasses and clusters of deep-green oaks. Then back to the book, reading each word, studying every graph and illustration of airplane performance, systems, and operations. I'm halfway through.

Helen finally arrives and takes the seat across from me. Without even greeting me, she reaches over and flips the book cover so she can read the title.

"*Airplane Flying Handbook*," she says. "Really?"

"Yeah."

"Is it ... I mean, are you understanding it?"

"I don't know. I think I am, but I guess I won't know until I'm actually, you know, *doing* it."

"So you signed up," she says, pleased.

"Well ... not exactly." I tell her about the grab-and-run. "When I got home and read about the classes, I just felt like such a beginner. I don't know *anything*. So I decided to read up on it before I go back. That way I'll have a little bit of an idea of what I'll be doing."

"It looks like you'll be able to build your own plane when you're done," she says. "You've highlighted every passage."

"I like to highlight."

"And when you finish it, you'll go back to the airfield, go inside, and sign up for lessons."

"Maybe. After another review …"

She frowns. "MJ, you see what you're doing here?"

"What?" I ask, but I know.

"You're wasting time! You need to just *do* this instead of sitting around highlighting passages. Life is short. Shorter than we know. Just start taking the lessons. Get on with it."

I sit back and look at her. "Hey," I say, "what's going on? You look exhausted."

"Nothing. Sorry if I snapped at you."

"Not nothing. Tell me."

"It's just that, I need to prioritize … with the new school year starting and all …"

"Don't tell me you signed up for more volunteering again!"

"No, not exactly something I volunteered for."

"Stop being mysterious. What does 'not exactly something' mean?"

"Waiting for—some news."

"What *kind* of news?"

"My energy's a bit low. Probably just a low thyroid level. No big deal."

In my gut, a sudden clenching; this feels ominous. Her casual "no big deal" doesn't match the look in her eyes. "When will you find out?"

"In a couple of days, probably."

"And you'll let me know the minute you hear?"

"Of course. So enough about me. You'll let me know about your lessons? I'll expect to hear about them in another couple of days too."

"Sure. Of course. In a couple of days."

"I'm holding you to it. Skim the rest of your book, and then go sign up. Promise me."

I nod dutifully. "I promise."

If only I hadn't promised. But after more than four decades of imagining it, I pull into a parking place of a flight school. I turn off the motor and look around.

Small airplanes wait in neat rows under the canopy of a blue, morning sky. A few guys are walking with a confident gait toward the airplanes. They have the "I-know-what-I'm-doing" look that reminds me of how much I don't know what *I'm* doing. I feel like a college freshman, looking at the upper classmen. I have to get out of my car. *Ready … now.*

Inside the lobby a counter separates me from the office staff. Pictures of aircraft of all vintages adorn the walls—from open cockpits with white, scarf-wearing pilots to sleek business jets with pilots flashing bright smiles.

In the middle of all this hangs a glassy-eyed sailfish in taxidermic stasis. I'm wondering why when a voice blares over an intercom, saying something about his airplane needing fuel. Someone at the desk answers on her handheld microphone that a fuel truck is on its way.

"Help you?" asks one of the other women behind the desk.

"Yes. I'd like to … I'm here to … to schedule lessons. Flying lessons."

"Great. We have classes starting next week."

"Well … I guess I could have my highlighting done by next week."

"I'm sorry?"

"Next week is fine."

She nods. "Next week. And the lessons are for …?"

"For … me."

"Good! We can use more women in our classes. Okay, let's see. The instructor for your flight and ground lessons is Will."

I picture what Will looks like: older, a retired commercial airline captain, grey hair, a million hours of flight time. "He's been flying for a while?"

"Yes."

I fill out some forms, and then she hands me a different textbook on aviation, assorted study guides, and my first assignment. With a shaking hand, I take out my calendar and write the date—a week from today. All the while I'm excited and scared and staggered at my courage and thinking, *I'm doing it! I'm really doing it! I can't believe I'm doing it!*

I thank her and turn to leave, and nearly bump into a young man with bright eyes.

"My student called in sick," he says, "so 83Bravo is available in case anyone wants a lesson in it."

"What luck," says the woman. "MJ, this is Will, your instructor. Want to take a look at the airplane you'll be flying?"

The airplane I'll be flying? I freeze. No! I'm not ready!

"MJ? Nice to meet you." His handshake is sort of a pull toward him. "Come on."

I glance in alarm at the woman behind the desk, and she delivers an encouraging nod.

Following Will, I mumble, "Okay. Sure."

"I spent a few years in the military," he says, "and I just got myself a new sports car. See?" He points to a shiny new Z.

"Very nice. I learned to drive a stick on a Z." A sudden Mrs. Robinson moment; no need to tell him it was probably before he was born.

What I like about him already is that he's obviously happy to give me a lesson. We walk out to the ramp, and he points to the airplanes and talks about their differences in power and performance. From multiple pockets on his khaki jumpsuit come paper, pens, sunglasses—plus something he pops in his mouth.

"Peppermint?" he offers. "Always keeps a settled stomach in the skies."

"Thanks." I make a note to buy some.

"Here's your airplane," he says, beaming, patting the side of it like it's a thoroughbred. "Meet Bravo."

My heart sinks. Not a hearty stallion but an old mare ready to be put out to pasture, Bravo has a faded red stripe running along its side, and the rest of the white part is pining for a coat of wax. The two-blade propeller is at rest. I run my fingers along its blades and move them up and down. I stand back and look again. It's an old VW bug—with wings. An old model Cessna 152.

"This can fly?" Gracefully, I disguise my dismay with a joke. "Where's the rest of it?"

He laughs. "A lot of great pilots—astronauts too—started in this very model. You can work up to bigger, faster ones in time. This one is great for starters."

I walk around the tired-looking beast. "Did you say astronauts?"

"Yup." He hands me a card that looks like a menu. "We start each flight with a checklist."

As he begins to recite parts, I recognize the names from my book: two wings, a tail, wheels, and a long fuselage onto which all are attached. Yes, this is indeed an airplane, confirmed by months of diligent highlighting.

"Will, when are airplanes ready for retirement?" I ask after seeing that Bravo's manufacturing date is the same year that "Stayin' Alive" was a big hit for the Bee Gees.

"Listen, she's old and sun-bleached, but her mechanic keeps the important parts in good shape," Will assures me. "Keep asking questions. I like that."

He opens the door, and it squeaks. The smell inside is—chocolate? That's inviting. The seats are red leather. The carpet, once also red, is now a collage of gray, black, brown. The inside front panel stares back at me, mute now, but is the compact collection of gauges that are its storytellers. These gauges tell how fast, how high, what directions (turning, up, down, straight), and how the tail swings with each turn.

I reach out to gently touch the rim of a gauge, mostly out of wonder. I'm finally meeting the faces I've read so much about and that communicate the airplane's ever-changing motion. They tell the story, but I must read that story correctly, minute by minute.

"Someday, you'll get this craft checked out, up in the air, and return it back to the runway by yourself. It'll be a magical moment. You'll see."

I nod. Yeah, sure.

We stand before one another—the airplane and I. A slight breeze rocks its wings.

"So," Will says, "want to bring her to life?"

"More than anything," I admit.

"Let's do it."

We get in. I put on the headset, and the fast banter sounds serious.

"Can you hear me?" Will asks through his headset.

"Yes. But mostly all the other ... talking."

"The language of the sky. You'll learn to listen to it and filter out what's important." His seat is only inches from mine. I can hear the peppermint crunch too and, looking to my right, see his jaws working on it even as he talks. "I'll handle all the communication."

"Thank you," I say, relieved. Their deep voices, like auctioneers, begin and end their messages with letters and numbers. I should have read more about this.

"Clear!" yells Will from his open window.

The propeller shudders and comes alive, spinning, and the roar from the engine announces surprising power from such a small machine. The sleeping craft awakens and kicks like a filly that's been pent up. Will adjusts the gauges as the needles inside bounce to their positions in response. This is not a book; it's what the words meant—and way more exciting.

"As we move, use the rudders to steer her taxi," Will says.

"Me?"

"Yeah. Go ahead."

With a total lack of grace I weave down the taxiway, past the control tower, and down to meet the end runway that we're cleared to use.

"I'm awful at this," I say, disappointed.

"You'll get better with practice. Little touches on the pedals. Look at the yellow line."

"Yellow line? I'm watching for other airplanes."

I bring us to a stop before entering the runway.

"You follow along with a light touch on the controls. I'll do the flying. You can tell a lot about a person, you know, by the way they control the yoke of an airplane."

"How?"

"In their touch. Men who do physical jobs, like heavy lifting, hold too tightly. You do something more cerebral, I bet, like reading or writing. Yours is softer."

"How should it be?"

"You change it as needed. You'll learn."

"I appreciate your confidence."

The large painted numbers on the runway, 19R, loom in size compared to our airplane. I could fit the whole plane on the number 1. We align the plane at the foot of the numbers. The control tower says something about the runway. Will rattles off an agreement and direction.

"I never get tired of takeoffs," I hear him say through his headset to mine. "Here it comes."

He gives Bravo a full, steady throttle, and the little airplane quickens its pace until it practically lifts itself into the sky. Earth falls smoothly away as hangars and airplanes I passed moments ago grow smaller.

He explains how to make a turn, points out other distant airfields, and chatters into his headset to voices coming through. I hear sounds, even a short laugh, but it's like the language of a foreign land.

"How do you do all this, Will? Fly, talk, listen?"

"You'll be able to do it too." He looks outside, his hands and feet working. "Here's where we turn. Now you'll see it. *Really* see it."

The airplane's gauge says we have reached 3,000 feet. He pushes down the nose of the craft to level our flight, toward the landmarks of horizons west, rolling hills with high-shouldered headlands. Turning wide, owning the full skyline to the east, the bold Sierra, with clouds resting along its back.

Delta waters, making their way to join oceans and tides, sparkle and blink while heron wing their way above them. Roads trace paths from city to farmlands. All below is in quiet connection.

Above all this, we fly in a craft built only, I'd thought, to take us to other runways. We skate along the air, between clouds and hills, and I'm seeing Earth for what feels like the first time.

"Want to take her?" Will asks.

"Now?" I'm terrified, but … *yes*.

"Follow that road. Down there," he tells me and gives me the controls. "Your airplane. You reply: 'My airplane.'"

"My airplane."

"Your airplane. Good. And … does *your* airplane seem too small now?"

I blush. The wings jerk left and right, responding to my not-so-gentle grip. I look at the road below along the open countryside, then smooth out the way to trace it from above. Time has left me.

Too soon, Will requests the controls. "We need to get back."

"Can I ask you something? Does the magic last? Or is it just on the first lesson?"

"It lasts. For me, anyway."

I close my eyes and inhale it all. "Good."

Will calls in to land and shows me what it takes to make a flying machine return to an earthbound existence and be silent again.

We get out, and with checklists stored and wings firmly tied to the ground, he says, "I'll show you around. Then show you your study material. I know, I know. Studying is what student pilots hate most."

Before I follow him back inside, I whisper to my airplane, "I'm sorry. I was wrong."

That night at dinner I announce my unexpected first lesson. Jim and Blake are delighted, but Annie is surprisingly quiet.

"Of course you knew most of it," Blake says. "You studied it a ton."

"I studied the *pieces*. There's way more to it than what's in the book. Now it's time to connect all the dots."

"How many dots do you have to connect?" Annie asks.

"Maybe a thousand."

"Wow, that's a lot," she says.

Later, she and I are left alone to do the dishes. She's not working at her usual brisk pace, and I hear her sigh.

"You okay?"

"Fine. Except …" She shrugs.

"Except what? Did something happen at school?"

"It's just that I was really excited to tell my friends that you're going to be flying planes, but then Arney's mom, she was standing there, and she said, 'Well, that's just crazy!' All I did was walk away, but I wanted to kick her. Why did she say that? Is it crazy, Mom? What you're doing?"

Knowing Arney's mom, I'm not surprised to hear her take on this. An unremarkable bore if ever there was one.

I laugh it off. "I guess she doesn't know much about flying. There's nothing crazy about it. I'm very, very careful. I won't be taking chances or flying on my own until everything says I'm really ready. Like Blake said, 'I'm studying it tons.' You know that, right?"

"I guess so."

"Arney's mom was wrong to say that to you, but she didn't mean to scare you."

"She called you a name."

"Yeah, that wasn't very nice."

"I wanted to call her a name back!"

"No, name-calling is never right. As a matter of fact, today I called the airplane a name. And I was wrong."

"The airplane? What did you call it?"

"I said it was too small. But then I went up, and—"

"Too small? Girls at school say that about me. And they laugh. You know …" She gestures at her chest. "*Here.* Some of them are already growing. When's it going to happen for me?"

The conversation had been going smoothly until this bit of turbulence. How to answer?

Just then Blake comes into the kitchen. "Put Kleenex in your bra," he suggests. "That's what some girls do."

Whoa. "How do you know that?"

"I saw a girl on a TV show do it."

Annie's eyes are huge, going from my face, to Blake's, back to mine.

"It's an old trick," I tell her.

"Did *you* do it, Mom?"

"Sure," I say, "and what I found was that, if I took the Kleenex out of the box first, I got a much better shape."

Blake and I laugh. Offended and humiliated, Annie runs out, and I hear her tearing up the stairs.

I go after her and find her curled up with her plush bunny, his fur worn thin from years of love. I put my arm around her.

47

"Lovey, I really do understand how you feel."

She moans into her bunny, "I hate school."

"Yours will grow—I promise."

"Oh, I don't care about that. I just don't want anyone calling you crazy. Even another mom. If she does that again, I'm going to call *her* something. Maybe 'fat.' She is, you know."

"Don't stoop to her level, Annie," I say, but at the same time I'm again questioning my decision to fly. I can take someone calling me crazy, but why should my daughter have to deal with that?

The Scent of Flying

NOT SURPRISINGLY, I am the only woman. My classmates are Tom, John, and Henry. All early 20s, distracted by the sound of airplanes taking off outside but with a casual attitude about the whole scene. Then there's me: overly diligent, extremely well versed on the written material, and looking like a housemother who crashed a fraternity party. The one who brings snacks. Will is an easy-going instructor, calm and patient. Within a week we are all good friends.

"Hey, MJ. What did you do over the weekend?" asks Tom before class begins.

"Studied. Then we took our kids to the science museum in the city. Lots of fun. How about you?"

"I just started dating this really cool girl, and we, you know, hung out."

Henry hurries in. With hair uncombed and shirttail half untucked, he falls into the seat next to me. "She's wearing me out," he says, referring to his girlfriend. "But totally turned on being with a pilot."

"Ha!" John gives him a shove. "She's with someone else then. You're only a *student* pilot."

"Shut up, you ass ..." Henry looks at me. "Oh. Sorry, MJ. Hey, so ..." He lowers his voice and leans close. "Did you happen to do the homework? Could I take a quick look?"

I carefully lift the neatly completed page from my binder and offer it to him. He grabs it and copies down some answers.

"Thanks. Hey, I didn't get a chance to have breakfast. Did you by any chance bring in something to eat?"

"Cookies," said Tom, handing him the now nearly empty bag.

Will, who witnessed the copying, shakes his head. "Homework is one thing, guys, but you all need to start studying for your FAA [Federal Aviation Administration] written exam. Lots to know." He sits on the corner of his desk and continues. "Our topic today is one each of you will practice with me. On your flight lesson. We're going to learn about stalls and falls. It's the first maneuver to do because it's a leading cause of accidents and de ... well, bad stuff." He gets up and draws a wing on the whiteboard, with lines for air traveling over it. "You will understand stalls, why they happen, and how to get out of them. You will all be stall masters."

I've read about stalls and am rightly afraid of them: airplane falling out of the sky, like a duck shot down by a hunter. If a stall happens and is not resolved in time, it's most likely the last day for both pilot and plane.

Will asks, "Why does an airplane stall? John?"

"Because it loses ... the right wind around the bottom of its wings. And around the top." John frowns and adjusts his new sunglasses, which perch jauntily on his head. He's leather and coolness. He definitely looks the part.

"MJ?"

Blinking away from the jacket, I look back up at Will. "Stalls. Happen when," I say, checking my notes, "the wing has exceeded the—angle of attack. The wing has to meet the wind inside that area."

"Nice job."

So what. I sink down a little in my chair, feeling the eyes of the others turn my way. A book's definition. I don't really know what it means to fly one. I try to recall the steps in a stall maneuver but don't have them memorized.

"Care to draw the details of that relationship for us, Henry, with that sketch you just made?" asks Will.

Henry goes to the board with the drawing he copied from my homework. "Thanks," he whispers, and playfully punches me on his way up to the board.

We go through a few more questions and answers, then Will says it's time to practice. "MJ, you're first."

Stalls. "Right," I grin. *Crap.*

I've practiced the steps in my head, but how will it feel and sound and look in reality? I pop a peppermint as I follow Will out to the plane.

For a few minutes he quizzes me while I check the condition of the airplane: "What if you find water in the fuel tanks? How do you know the tires can take another landing? If something is broken, does it matter? Can you still legally take off?"

To fly right means being dedicated to learning everything, from the drops of oil inside the plane to the drops that come from the clouds above.

"One day, just this machine and you will be in the air," Will always says. That's motivation enough for me to want to know every droplet.

What is endearing about Bravo is its mix of interior aromas: aviation fuel (sweet kerosene) and leather. And chocolate—the mechanics drink lots of hot chocolate to stave off the chill of the hangar as they work on the airplanes. Collectively, they are the scent of flying and add to my anticipation that the sky is coming.

I have already improved at some things. "You're much better at keeping the seat belt from getting stuck in the door," Will teases. "And your taxiing! Got that front-nose wheel right on the yellow taxi line!"

Although we have headsets, we both need to talk loudly to be heard. Once airborne, he says, "I'm going to level the plane at 5,000 feet. Before we learn how to get out of a stall, let's see what it takes to get in one."

I nod, concentrating.

"Pull the power out. Carb heat goes in. Bring the nose up. Feel the mush as the wings lose lift. Lifting. Lifting. Higher. And always, *always*, stay on the rudder pedals to maintain coordination."

The airplane goes nose high. A stall warning horn blasts throughout the cabin. Bravo sounds like it's dying, its proud, powerful hum gone. It's out of its safe angle to the wind. The nose blows to the left and pitches down, unable to stand it anymore. *We're falling.*

"Now to recover flight, quick and clean. Power in. Carb heat out. Nose down. Keep the wings level. Bring the nose slightly higher ..." Will reconfigures the airplane, and Bravo is resuscitated. An airplane brought to life again. He recovers the airplane without much altitude lost. "Your turn."

I swallow, pop another peppermint. "I made a note card of the steps to get into one and recover," I say. "Can I look at it?"

"This time. But memorize all the steps. You'll need to know more than a dozen other maneuvers and *all* the steps. Start memorizing!"

I tuck the little white card under the band of a small clipboard attached by Velcro around my thigh. Small aircraft are cramped, so space is used as efficiently as possible. Deep breath. Lift the nose to the sky. Keep peeking at my card. Hear the scream of the airplane, which could just as well be mine. Recover to bring the wind back to the wings, losing about 500 feet of altitude.

"Hey!" I hear myself exclaim. "Still alive!"

"Good start. Too much altitude lost," he says. "Just the few extra seconds to look at your notes can do that. You'll practice these a lot on your own when you're signed off to do solo practices. Then you'll do one for the examiner on your final test."

I'm happy. Bravo skims along, strong again, in the cloudless, blue sky.

Back in class, the guys cheer my return.

"How was it?" asks Tom.

"The horizon's—gone. You go straight up. Then down."

"It's awesome that you did it! My mom never would."

"My mom can't drive her car," John says.

Do all these guys still live at home? Well, now they have two mothers—the ones at home doing their laundry and the one at the airfield helping them with their homework and giving them cookies.

"Got your calls" is Helen's message on my machine when I get home. "Really busy here. Uh, company and all that. I'll call as soon as I ... can."

Disappointed, I think it's business as usual for her—taking on too many volunteer assignments despite our vow to cut back in order to pursue something more meaningful.

I shrug off my coat and flight bag and sit at my kitchen table. It's become an airfield where toy airplanes are parked around a growing array of classroom material.

For the next class, we will be called upon to describe the features of a naturally aspirated engine and diagram how a carburetor can freeze in warm weather. The next class is on airplane limits, drawing the inside systems of an airplane's fuel line, how the six-pack gauges work and why sometimes they don't, and what a pilot must do in the event of an emergency.

For this is the dark side of flying: Stuff fails. To prevent my family from worrying about me—or worse yet, to keep Jim from thinking it's as bad as helicopters—I do the worst-case-scenario studying to myself. I've made the first of several kinds of checklist flashcards to memorize while waiting in the car, while stirring dinner on the stove, or while standing at the back of the room at scout meetings.

Some of the books from our classroom contain horrifying pictures of crumpled wings—examples meant to warn us new flyers about the outcomes of bad decisions. Like planning to get married and reading stories about painful divorces. Not inspired by devastating endings, I mostly read how it's supposed to work and how to fix it.

Later that week an early winter storm stretches on for days, keeping me grounded. Rain taps for help in code on windowpanes, but the wind continues to lash. I think of the sheets of rain racing down the runways and hope Bravo has been tied down well enough.

As the hour heads to midnight, I sit by our fireplace, deciphering the latest chapter on pitch and power until I can't keep my eyes open. I feel like I can't even think straight. Last week I forgot to bring cupcakes to school as I had promised. *I'm slipping.* I had expected flying to be exhilarating and scary, but I had truly not anticipated all the hours of work required. I can't even remember the last time I slept more than four hours.

I'm concerned about Annie too. She hasn't mentioned any more problems with mothers thinking I'm crazy, but knowing her she might have and decided to keep it to herself so that my feelings wouldn't be hurt.

"I don't like all this airplane stuff," announces a little voice grimly, and I open my eyes to see Blake standing in front of me. He looks half angry and half hurt. "You're always reading now. You're always flying."

An echo of thunder fades into the distance.

"I suppose it sort of looks that way," I say, slowly closing my book and furtively sliding a toy airplane under a pillow.

"I don't get to see you much now."

"Oh, Blake, you'll always come before flying." I pat the sofa cushion next to me. He hops up and four notebooks slide to the floor, sending papers in disarray. I resist picking them up. "I study as much as I do because almost all of it is new to me. But I keep trying."

"Aren't you the top student?"

"No." I shake my head. "Not the top. Just a hard worker."

"How are the other moms in your class doing?"

"I'm the only one—so far."

"Maybe, do you think this might be, you know, a phase you're going through?"

"A *phase*?"

"Yeah. I hear that sometimes moms have them."

"Have you been talking to Dad?"

He shifts. "Well ..."

"No, this is *not* a phase."

"So how come you do it? What do you like about it so much?"

"It's something I've wanted to do. My whole life. Since I was your age. A long time."

"So, what's it like?"

"Well, every time I climb into Bravo ..."

"The airplane has a name?"

"Yes. Based on the numbers and letters assigned to it."

A number lover, he's interested now.

"I climb in, snap together my seat belt and harness, and put on my headset. Now Bravo and I are like one. Then I pop a peppermint and start."

"What does the peppermint have to do with it?"

"It adds a taste of courage. Then I start the engine and look at the oil pressure. When the prop kicks in, the needles in the gauges dance a bit before they settle on what to point at. Then I turn up my headset so I can hear what the people in the tower and other pilots are saying. In mostly deep, fast voices."

"Like this?" Blake babbles something in a low voice.

"Yes, like that. About which airplanes are taking off and which are landing. Weather conditions. Everything is constantly moving, changing."

He uses his hand as an airplane that takes off and rises above his head.

"Then, there's a moment of ... it's ... magic. I feel myself leave Earth, rising higher and higher, while everything familiar and below gets smaller. The rivers, all the cars ... the roads are black snakes. The mountains share the air at my level. I am circling in wonder and grace. A sense of forever. Of infinity." Just saying the words aloud makes me stop.

His airplane hand stops in midair. "Go on."

"I like getting the airplane to turn and climb, and I love when I get it just right, though I'm not perfect most of the time. And when the flight is over, it lingers in my heart long after. I whisper my thanks to Bravo for taking me, as I wipe off her propeller."

Blake lands, saying, "Good plane."

"Still, I love you and Annie even more." I put my arm around him, and the two of us sit silently on the sofa for a while, as dancing patterns from the fireplace play on the walls and the storm outside buffets the world.

"I sort of thought it was like that," he says eventually. "Do you think the airplane knows how you feel? About flying it?"

"Maybe."

A flash of lightning leaves its signature across the dark sky. Blake knows more about the meaning of flying than my textbooks tell me. Flight touches my soul more than anything else, except for my family.

"How many books will it take?"

I sigh, reminded of the work ahead of me. "Lots. I tell you what: When I get my license, you and I will go on a flight together. I know of a great lunch place on the runways at Napa. How does that sound?"

He nods. We listen to the commotion outside.

"Mom? Will you fly in storms? Like this one?"

In the howling wind I detect the faint sound of a jet overhead, changing its usual course to battle wind and rain on its way into San Francisco International, 30 miles away.

"I won't fly in storms. I'm not looking for fights, just fair skies and mild breezes," I assure him. "If the weather makes birds tumble and their feathers blast off, then it's not a flying day for me either."

He laughs quietly. "Good. Oh, hey." He shifts in his seat, then hands me the toy airplane from under the cushion. "I think this is yours."

"Have you heard from Helen?" asks Joan, who asked me to drop by after my flight class.

"I keep leaving messages. She's called back once or twice, leaving messages about how busy she is but will call back soon. Not like her."

"She was … waiting to hear about some … tests. Did she tell you too?"

"Yes. Now weeks have gone by. But hopefully no news is good news."

"I have a feeling it's bad news," Joan says. "I might have to drop by to see her. Casually. I-happen-to-be-in-the-neighborhood kind of thing. That usually works, even if it is transparent."

"Good plan. Maybe we're getting nervous over nothing."

"I hope." Joan cuts into her magazine-perfect cinnamon cake.

"I already know I want to have the entire thing," I say. "Let me take it. I'll bring some to the school to make up for the cupcakes I forgot."

"What a compliment," she says, as she puts a generous slice on my plate.

"Joan, this is …," closing my eyes just so I can dwell on it, "superb."

"Thanks."

"I went to a fund-raiser the other day. What they served was not anywhere near as good as this, and they specifically said their bakery was the best. You'd put them out of business."

She smiles, pleased.

"But," I go on, "when I was there, I ran into Fran."

"Uh oh."

"What's the first thing she says? 'Are you still flying?' in a high, are-you-still-doing-that-ridiculous-thing voice."

"You should have told her to mind her own business."

"So I tell her I am." I gesture at my plate. "Seriously. How do you do this? I know it must be with the best butter, but it tastes lighter than air!"

"Just a great recipe. It's what buns that aren't *burnt* taste like," she says, winking at me. "Fran's the one who dresses like her teenage daughter, right?"

"That's Fran."

"Not that I have anything against a woman our age trying to look good," Joan amends. She knows she is guilty of using every tool in the shed: hair dye, lots of makeup, manicures, pedicures, skin peels, teeth whiteners. "Anyway, what did she say?"

"She said, with insincere sweetness, 'You know, I'm only asking out of concern. My brother had friends who were pilots.' So I say, 'Great. What did they fly?' And she says, 'I have no idea—they all died flying them.' She's got a friend with her, and her friend is giving me a doubtful look. Had they previously discussed this, to warn me of my doom? Since they are *so* concerned? Probably that's what they'll say at my funeral: 'We *told* her not to do it!'"

"Well, I sort of said that too, that it was crazy. At first I did. But now I think it's great," says Joan. "I'm sorry. How'd you get away from her?"

"The best part is coming. I change the subject and ask what she's been up to, and she starts listing house and school things. I know it all too well from my old planners that I didn't even listen, to be honest, until she says, 'It must be nice to have time to take flying lessons. Jim working so hard and all.'"

"She didn't say that!"

"Did. Then the final kicker: guilt. Asking me how I can *do that* to Jim and our family."

"What a bitch. She has no idea. No right to say that to you. She doesn't get it."

"She will *never* get it. Even worse, not ever *want* to get it!" I stand to try to release the tension and calm my breathing. Fran's conceit digs deeper in me. "I know I shouldn't let her get to me."

"You acted like a real pro," Joan says. "You had plenty of reasons to let her know what a jerk she is."

"She would rather be right and see me dead than know what it means to have such a passion. *Any* passion. She doesn't know. She resents it so much that she forbids herself to be happy for me!"

Joan sits, staring at me, waiting until I finish railing. I am panting with anger. Done, I sit, drained, and put my hands on my head and feel my curls more tangled than usual from the headset I wore while flying earlier. *I must look a mess.*

"Sorry. It was a difficult lesson this morning. I'm tired. I started learning a new maneuver. I haven't gotten it down. Not yet."

"I'm glad you told me," says Joan gently. "If that's what airplane rhapsody tastes like, I'd have a piece of *that*. That is, if I weren't already so busy keeping Roger happy."

"I guess I should feel sorry for Fran. She's … stuck."

"I know what you mean. She's also really angry," murmurs Joan. "Sometimes I feel that way."

"Why?"

"Nothing," Joan says, blinking. "So, other than that, what did they serve at the function?"

We laugh, finish the cake, and talk about Joan's latest fashions, bomber jackets at the flight school, and other cool looks.

"Joan," I say, licking my fingertips, "seriously, have you ever thought of starting a business?"

"A business? No. That's *crazy*. Never. Like what?"

"Like …," I gesture at the plate that now holds just crumbs, "… what you bake better than anyone else?"

"Roger would never allow it."

On my way home I turn on my talk radio station and hear the host ask, "It's been on the decline for *how* long?"

"Our research," answers the guest, "shows that it's been going down for several years now."

"But why? What is keeping women from being happy? There've been so many advances … more opportunities … education. Isn't any of that helping?"

"Contradictory to expectations, none of those factors guaranteed happiness. Neither did useful, modern gadgets designed to save time and make life easier."

"What is it then? Are they looking for more in life, do you suppose? Is Betty Friedan's comment from decades ago still relevant today?"

"It appears so. But more studies are needed to help us determine what the key elements are. After all, research tells us that happiness is critical to long life."

"Well, *that's* for sure! Thanks for joining us today," says the host.

I shut off the radio. If happiness is associated with a long life, then unhappiness shortens life. Right?

That night, I call Helen. As usual, her machine picks up.

"Helen," I say in a stern voice, "I'm worried. I want to know what's going on. Please call me when you—"

She surprises me by picking up. "I'm here. Sorry."

"What the hell is going on?"

"It's been … a tough time."

"You told me you'd call," I say dryly. "You disappeared. Company with you or not, you *told* me …"

"How's flying?"

"A lot of work. Now tell me what's going on."

On her end, a little choking sound.

"Can you tell me … those tests … what's going on?"

"It's bad news, MJ."

"Oh, no."

"I wanted to tell you in person … but … it's cancer. Maybe the next time you're free, you could stop by …"

"I'm on my way," I say, and hang up before she can tell me not to come.

Prop Me Up

I RAP GENTLY ON HELEN'S DOOR, thinking a quiet touch is better than the every-occasion blaring bell or a here-I-am-but-scared-as-hell knock. She opens the door, and for a moment we just stand there, looking at each other. Then she turns, and I follow her in.

"Helen, how are …"

"Furious! *That's* how I am! I just finished calling my cousins. They're 'stunned' and said, 'No one has had breast cancer in our family before.'"

She drops onto the sofa, and I sit next to her. "Why tell me that? Do they think I want to be the first? One actually asked, 'How do you think it happened?'"

"Oh, Helen …"

"How the hell do *I* know how cancer happens? Why not ask me how I'm feeling? They're just … about them."

"How *are* you fee …"

"They make it sound like I did something to bring this on. Like I've been reckless, or it's payback for some impure act I did in my past. They want me to tell them—*what*? How I *caught* it? So *they* won't get it?"

I wait while she catches her breath. I must keep myself together, for her sake, when I feel like raging too—over the injustice, the randomness. "When did you find out?"

"One week and six days ago. Just when my life was, you know, getting back to life after my parents died."

I nod. When her parents were killed in a car accident, she tripled her volunteer time as a way to deal—"To be too busy to dwell on it or think," she'd said.

"I had a mammogram," she goes on, "and the doctor told me there was something he wanted to take a closer look at, but most likely it was nothing to worry about. And I thought I'd already had enough bad news just last year. It wasn't my turn again, was it? And then I got the call."

My heart feels like it's breaking. Helen, who shares so much of her time helping others. Who is so good. I take her hand and listen.

"My doctor said, 'Actually, it's cancer.' Like he was kind of surprised too. I didn't say anything. Thankfully Brad was standing in the kitchen with me. I just gave him the phone and told him to take the call. 'It's the doctor. Talk to him.' Then I just walked outside. Numb. Thinking, 'How can this be real?'"

"How are you doing—now?" I ask meekly, but it sounds shallow. It's so obvious but a starting place.

"I'm ..." she pauses. "I'm pissed. At everything. After finally getting my feet back on the ground again! And I have two children." She wipes away tears. "I don't *need* this! And I hate their questions because I also wonder how it's in me. Maybe I *did* do something. Ate something, smoked something, drank too much. Or ..." her voice goes low, "maybe God is mad at me."

"You didn't *do* anything to get cancer, Helen. And God isn't mad at you." I want to scream against believing that disease is the penalty dealt out by an angry God who gets personally offended and torments our already short ride. But this is no time to confront the faith that means so much to her.

"Well, then, why do I feel like I screwed up?"

"Shit happens. Even to good people."

"Shit happens," she scoffs, hanging her head.

"Where's Brad? The children?"

"Asleep."

"How are they?"

"They're doing okay. I act like it's no big deal, so they're pretty calm. But when everyone goes to bed and I'm alone, I panic."

"Come on. Let's get out of here."

"What? Now?"

"Yeah." I stand. "Right now."

We go to a restaurant where the bar is off to the side, but the solo guitarist in the dining room can still be heard. The lights are kind, golden and soft, and in the mirror I see a glow that makes us look younger.

"Life used to be so easy," he says. "Like when this music was new." His guitar strums us back to the '70s with the Eagles, Steely Dan, Chicago, Kenny Loggins—a time when we were dreaming of going to college, of growing up, of having our whole lives ahead.

"So what happens now, Helen?"

"It's aggressive, unfortunately. I'm … that is, we're talking to my doctors and getting opinions. It looks like … it looks like it'll be a double mastectomy, radiation, chemo. The whole bag. Damn thing is at an advanced stage."

"Oh … god …"

"Don't you *dare* cry! I'm telling you because this will take a while, several months. I'm okay for now. Brad is trying to look strong, but I see how it hurts him. The other night he got up and stood in the girls' doorway to watch them sleep. When I came up to put my arm around him, he rubbed his eyes." Helen takes a couple of sips of chardonnay. "He's such a sweet guy. The girls love drawing him pictures that he puts in his office, of the four of us. What I want more than anything is to stay in those pictures. In those drawings he's smiling and looks so tall and handsome."

"Are you talking about me?"

A good-looking man with a loosened tie and rolled-up sleeves appears at our table. His hair is full and wavy, a little grey, and he's got his sights on Helen, of course. Even now she is sparkling. Her long, brown hair graces the dimples that frame the smile she wears wherever she goes. If we were both single, I'd hang out with her to meet all the ones left waiting in line.

"No," she snaps. "Beat it."

Startled, I stare at her. Used to be she'd be more polite—tell him to go away but more gently, chuckle ruefully, show her wedding ring, and say. "Thanks, anyway."

He holds up his palms in surrender and walks away, shaking his head.

"How *dare* he," she sputters.

"Because you're so pretty, Helen ..."

"Think a guy like that will come over to me after I've lost my hair? You lose your eyelashes too, you know. And your eyebrows." She finishes her wine and signals to the waitress that she'd like another. "Your pupil, or public ... pubic hair too." The alcohol is quickly giving her a buzz. She's always been a lightweight. She furrows her brow, then closes her eyes. Her shoulders fall, and her hand goes up to her head.

The music from long ago continues.

When the waitress comes over, I tell her that I'll have another glass too. Then to Helen, I say, "You know, I'm here for you. How can I help?"

"Just put up with me. I need an easy, soft, safe spot. Listen, and excuse my rants."

"Any time. Joan will want to help too. Maybe we should change to the Chicks for Change."

"Too much change," she grumbles. "You know how you're doing so much in the air, and left me a message that said it was like seeing things for the first time? I've been thinking how there's so much I've been missing. So I've decided to simplify my life. No more endless meetings or school programs. I'm focused on my family. Happy to have each day, still surviving to see the next one."

"I won't bother you with any more crazy air stories then."

"No! I want to hear them all!"

"As long as they don't sound too trivial. Compared with what you're doing and feeling."

"What would make me angry is my friends not realizing what they have waiting for them."

"Any of us could have gotten your news. Or still might. One day. Who knows? Lives change from moment to moment."

"I'm taking in the moments of the day like I never have before. Like savoring a cup of tea. The children laughing. My favorite old sweater. The overlooked miracles."

We look at each other and, at the same moment, raise our glasses— clink! We're in a new season of our lives and our friendship. Deeper. But uncharted. And scary.

"How is your flying going? Still studying and highlighting like a mad woman? Have you gone up again?"

"Slicing up the sky with Will. Plus I have whole libraries now filled up with brightly lined pages." I stop, unsure if I should mention this now. But, if not now, I may miss the chance. I tell her about the dragon poem in my uncle's book, about facing fear or surrendering to it. "So I was thinking … maybe you and I could help each other outsmart our dragons. I know that the sky holds the place for mine. But for you, maybe we could learn about the illness together. And how to fight it."

"I don't want information. I just want it to go away! Let the doctors do the reading, do the highlighting. I refuse to acknowledge that it has any power to scare me. Or that it even exists. I want to walk through the treatment center like a ghost. Like I'm not really there at all. I'll save my real spirit for the rest of my time with the people I love."

"Sorry."

"No, don't apologize. It's a good idea. For you."

We hear the snap of the guitarist, who is locking his case, and the bar is calling it quits for the night. Without noticing, the hours have flown by.

"What time is it?"

I check my watch. "Midnight."

"Wow. I need to get back." Then she smiles. "When was the last time we were out this late, closing down a bar?"

"Long time."

Out in the still night air, I look up at the constellations and see Orion, playboy hunter, forever flirting with the lovely Pleiades ladies, who forever run away. But Orion is a sign that winter is coming. I feel a chill.

"Listen," says Helen, "highlight all you can, okay? I'm glad you study so hard. I don't want to lose you when you're flying by yourself and something—some dragon—comes out of the blue."

"You won't. Lose me, that is. I'll be alright."

"And another thing …"

"Yes?"

"Tell me what you discover about your dragon. Bring me your stories. Especially the ones about when the skies are beautiful and blue."

She's drunk, sentimental. Feels better, and actually so do I. Also I'm glad that I am driving, not her.

"You're going to be alright too," I say firmly.

Out the window I see my classmate Tom pull up in his motorcycle.

I see him and say as he comes in, "Shouldn't you have your leather jacket on? For the extra padding?"

"Too confining. I love the freedom. At least I wear a helmet. *Mom.*"

I want to say, "Don't take risks you don't need to take!" But I don't. What he's doing is what I call "teasing the dragon": pulling its tail when it already comes with plenty of danger.

We decipher our charts—their endless lines and circles of blue and magenta that provide safety information about heights and locations—by checking tops of mountains and towers, airport details, and Earth's changing magnetic influence on our compasses.

"I can't believe how hard I used to think decoding these symbols used to be," I say. "Now it's fascinating. It's like art." When Tom doesn't respond, I say, "You don't think so?"

"No one in my family knows I'm here."

"Studying charts?"

"No, I mean learning to fly airplanes."

"Really?"

"Really."

"But … why haven't you told them?"

"Because it's understood that I'll be going into the family business."

"Which is …?"

66

"The mortuary business. Funeral stuff."

"Oh."

"Yeah."

"Very different from taking it to the sky."

"Yeah. I make my money there and spend it here, on lessons."

"So what do you do?"

"Right now I'm the groundskeeper. But they want me to learn everything else. Then do it full time. For the *rest* of my *life*."

He's only 10 years older than Blake and still looks like a kid. His hair is tousled, and he has a congenial manner that makes him easy to like. I try to picture him digging graves … flinging shovels of dirt over his shoulder … pausing to squint at the sky as a plane flies overhead.

"That's a bummer."

"I know. All day I'm surrounded by dying. I want to do something that makes me feel alive. But my parents will never let me."

"So where do they think you go when you come here?"

"I tell 'em I'm going out for a ride."

"Won't they find out at some point?"

"I just don't know how to tell them." He taps the charts, then his face brightens. "Hey, you could help me. You're a mom *and* a pilot. How do you think I should tell them so they won't get mad?"

"Well, try thinking about it from your parents' viewpoint. Let's see. What could be useful to them?"

"To just work in the family business."

"No, I mean, is there a way you could convince them that an airplane is useful in the business? And you as their pilot? I mean, I can't imagine what, but …"

"Funny you mention that, MJ. Actually, there *is* something for a pilot to do."

"Great! What?"

"Dispersing ashes."

"Ashes?"

"Yeah. Over the ocean. And at sunset for a nice effect for those watching from the shore. I think there's big money in it."

67

"Oh. So, is it … legal? For ashes and everything to be flying out of an airplane?"

"Sure. You have to go out a distance from the shore," he says, pointing out to sea on our chart. "Then have a copilot dispense of them properly so they don't … ah, you know … blow back inside. Accidentally."

"Operator error," I say. "Occupational hazard. Checklists must be followed."

"Right. I'll think of a way to bring it up."

"You could even light the ashes. To make them look like meteors falling to Earth," I suggest, kidding.

"Great idea! So did you do the homework?"

I open my binder to the pages and push it across the table. "Let me know what they say."

Each maneuver in the sky is becoming a practice of physics accompanied by—if I do it right—elegance. Nose up, lose speed, turn before the wind shoves me too far, watch where the wing slices the sky, feel the speed return, see the world turn from mostly blue up to mostly brown down, and at the end know that's where I want to end up. Level. Throttle in. Graceful. Exhilarating. *Breathe.*

"Will," I say, "how will you know when I'm ready to fly alone?"

"When I can tell that you know enough. And then some."

"I want to know everything," I say. "Not just enough."

"That's a nice goal. But not realistic. Knowing enough and then some is huge. Keep your eyes wide open. There is always more."

"Will it be enough though? For those solo flights?"

"Yes. Remember to pay attention to your first priority: *Fly the plane.* There will be … let's say 'adventures' in your future. Unexpected. Surprising. Scary even. *Fly the plane.* Always stay focused on that because, at those times, you will likely be flying solo."

Helen's focused too: on being mindful of everything. "It lifts my spirits," she tells me, "but it's exhausting too."

I think of how many day-to-day activities I perform on autopilot. The other day in the grocery store I was waiting in line, studying my cards, and had no idea it was time for me to move forward until the woman behind me said, "*Excuse* me!"

"Still want to help me?" Helen asks.

"Of course. Tell me how."

"I'm going to take a yoga class. I want you to take it with me. To keep me going. Will you?"

Fit in one more thing? "Of course."

"Be aware," says the yoga instructor. "When we're aware of how we breathe, our vision will widen."

I think about my breathing, but then right away I think about asking Will how I should breathe while flying. He'll have thought about it already, I bet. I'm so fortunate to have him as my yoga master for flight.

"In the quietude you will find escape from your racing thoughts ..."

Oops! Stop, racing thoughts. Focus on breathing.

From other rooms I hear the chanting, "*Om, Om, Om.*"

In the peace of slower breathing I disappear into a dream: Running as fast as I can, I leap and spread my arms. The earth spins at my feet. Arms outstretched, I wheel around, excited to find that I've been joined by a myriad of beating wings, starting with dozens, then up to thousands of birds. Rushing up by the wind, we rise and dip together, like a single kite. Then the beating of their wings, like thunder, mounts. The birds become a single, dark cloud and fierce with fire-red eyes. They turn to chase me, and I must do something to escape this moving monster and quick. But what? Should I face them and fight? No. I decide to flee. Seeing a patch of sky above, I head toward it, relieved to leave the torrent of fear behind. Finding a long field, I start descending down, down. Then, before landing, I put my feet out to receive the ground. I open my eyes to shake off the visualization, relieved that the hour is over.

Helen and I thank the instructor and walk out of the room.

"You okay?" Helen asks. "You're supposed to look serene after a yoga class, and you don't."

"I did it wrong, I think. How can you radiate bliss when you've been haunted instead?"

"You are not doing it wrong," says a voice from behind. We turn to see the instructor, looking composed, peaceful, and somehow aware that I need her. "You are facing a fear wrong. I was watching you."

"I've had it before, this same vision," I tell her, "in dreams." I describe the thundering birds, the feeling of weakness.

"You're going from darkness to light. You are not weak. You're finding the light. That's strength."

"You mean, don't let them scare me?"

"Of course they're going to scare you. But feeling afraid is not *acting* afraid." And bowing, hands together to honor the light in each other, she says, "*Namaste*," and serenely glides off.

I hear Will's voice in my head: "Fly the plane."

"Thanks for coming in a little early," Will says the next day. "I have an announcement to make."

We wait expectantly. He looks uneasy, pushing at the floor with the toe of his boot and looking down instead of at us. "I've just been offered a big job to be the new flight instructor for a regional airline."

After a moment of shock and dismay, we force out words of congratulation. I was told that this happens a lot—instructors moving on when career opportunities knock. But I didn't expect it to happen to Will— or me. I feel like the right wing just fell off my airplane. John is rubbing his neck; Tom is tapping his pencil on his desk; Henry is late.

"Your new instructor is Captain Lee."

Will holds out his hand, and an older man with a tan, weather-worn face strides in with swaggering confidence. "Good morning!" he booms.

Captain?

With respectful attention, I sit up straight and alert and wait for the command to be *at ease*. He tells us that he has retired from almost 40 years in commercial aviation and, before that, the military. Which explains the stern, grey crew cut.

"Will has given me a rundown on what each of you has learned. But let's see what you *know*. MJ ..."

Sitting up even straighter, I swallow. "Yes?"

"Tell us the equation for lift." He positions himself at the board, chalk in hand, prepared to write what I say.

I glance around. The guys haven't moved a muscle. "May I refer to my notes ..." I ask, adding, "... Captain?"

"Certainly! Use all available resources as pilot in command. The rest of you, follow along with your own notes. And, if for some *reason* you don't have your work done, I have some airplanes outside that need to be washed. MJ, proceed."

Henry jogs in and takes his seat. He looks around, baffled.

"And Henry!" the captain bellows. "You're next to tell us why maneuvering flight can be fatal."

The dark shadow of a dragon has swept across the room, leaving a chill in its wake.

The Chicks—Their Pilot Projects

NIGHTTIME. MY HOUSE AND the world are asleep, but I am at my kitchen table with a small, metal airplane, practicing my landings with placemats lined up as runways.

"83Bravo cleared to land, 32Left. Cleared to land 32Left, 83Bravo," I mutter, playing both air traffic controller and pilot. Will told me that visualizing with mock setups is a practice that bolsters learning. While it may have value, I feel about four decades too old for it.

Somehow my children sense that their mother is playing with toys, and they peek from behind the stair railings. I picture them thinking, *Bet none of the other moms are doing this.*

Now that I have an audience, I ham it up a bit, replying to the tower like a valley girl: "Like, fer sure, tower!"

The control tower is suddenly manned by a cowboy. "Howdy, there. It's 32 time for you, little Bravo."

Blake and Annie find this irresistible and run down the stairs to sit with me. For a while they watch, then begin to offer suggestions for improvement. Helping Mom with her homework—what a switch.

"You mumble too much when you talk to the control tower," critiques Blake. "Make sure you speak clearly. They need to know it's you. I won't be up there to remind you, so you gotta remember." He makes me a Post-it note—"No mumbling!"—to use in the airplane. I promise to put it on the front panel.

"I like how smooth you were on that last landing, Mom," adds Annie. "Good job. And your wheel didn't get caught in the placemat that time."

"Practice makes perfect landings."

"Whoops," she says. "Almost forgot!" Sliding off her chair, she runs up the stairs, her little, bare feet going *pound pound pound*. When she returns she hands me a paper-towel wrapped gift. "I made you this in art class."

I open it and see a picture of a red-and-blue airplane and the word "FLY" in colored sand glued to a board.

"Annie! It's wonderful!"

She beams, but Blake rolls his eyes. "Let's try that again in a real voice," he directs. "Be serious now."

I do it again, this time to his liking. "Blake," I say, "I want you to be the first to know that one day I plan to go beyond airplanes."

"What do you mean *beyond* them?"

"Learning to land an airplane and read its gauges has inspired me. I want you to be the first to know that someday I will rise, seize it in both hands, and learn how the TV remote works."

"*Mo-om*. Let me hear you land again. Begin."

The next morning, I meet Helen at the coffee shop. She looks so weary.

"I plan out my days around each hour now," she says. "I'll be so glad when the surgery is over. Thank God I have you and Joan to help me with meals and visits—and, of course, my kids." She sighs. "I looked at my schedules before cancer. What a frenzied life of 'very busy.'"

"But each hour? Isn't that sort of the same?"

"Not at all. I plan each day the night before. Hour by hour. What I'll serve for breakfast. What will be in the lunch bags for my girls. When I'll stop for gas. Groceries. This break with you. It helps me focus on the details. Especially how beautiful and delicate each hour is," she says. "And it gives me some control over the craziness."

"What's the craziest part of it? I'd like to help."

"It's like a kettle drum. In the background of my head, when I least expect it, I hear the drum. Whenever the thought comes to mind of my condition. Of my family. I hear the drum. I think I might be going crazy."

"Helen, what about the company of others who know what it's like to hear that big drum? I bet there's a group of ..."

"I don't want to think about joining anything. I've spent too much of my life in groups."

"But this time, it's for *you*. Not the school. Not a fund-raiser ... hey, what about Joan?"

"What *about* her?"

"She told me there are groups at her church. Support groups. She hasn't said in so many words, but I think she goes to some of them. Should I call her?"

"No. Well, I'm not so sure. What if I don't like it? I won't stay if I don't like it."

"Of course not," I say. "Just test them out. No contracts."

"I'll try it."

"Good!"

"On one condition. You come too."

No! Not that! I hate enclosed places where lots of people go who don't feel well. Filled with sadness. Filled with pain. But she has never asked anything of me before, not this important. "Okay. When?"

"After my surgery. When I get back on my feet. In a few weeks or so."

I smile encouragingly. For both of us.

While we wait for word from Brad about how the surgery went, I show Joan the schedule I've made for dinners, visits, some doctors' appointments, and help with Helen's children.

"When I get worried, I get organized," I say.

"Nice."

"I included the group meetings at your church that Helen and I are going to."

"I've asked for so many candles to be lit for her that I'm afraid the church will burn down," Joan jokes.

"Do you go there a lot? I didn't know you were so—faithful."

"It helps me set some priorities. That's what the Chicks in Charge are supposed to do. Right?"

Before I can say "right" back, the phone rings.

"Brad," I say, and answer. Break into a grin and give Joan a *thumbs up* as Brad says, "The surgery went great. She's resting."

Joan mouths, "Can we come see her?"

"Can we come see her?"

"Maybe a bit later. The surgery took longer than expected."

I'm hoping he'll explain why, but when he doesn't, I don't probe. "Okay, we'll hang around here for a while. Thanks so much for the update." I hang up and relay the news to Joan.

Joan lets out a deep breath. "So, should we worry that it took longer than expected?"

"No, but I will anyway."

"Me too. I wish we could go right now. Even if she's asleep. I want to see her."

"I do too, even though I hate those places. I feel like I need to hold her hand."

Joan has suddenly noticed the books about breast cancer on my table. "You're reading up on that too?"

"I want to understand what's going on. And I promised her I'd go to the meetings with her."

"MJ," Joan says quietly, "You know … you don't have to know *all* the answers. You know that, right?"

"I … what?"

"Helen doesn't need an expert right now. She needs a friend. Support. Be her copilot. Be behind her, and let her lead the way."

"I'm *letting* her lead the way," I protest. At the same time, I think, *What do you mean? Of course I have to have answers!*

"Do you ever wonder …" she pauses delicately.

"Wonder what?"

"Of this … obsession with highlighting and studying … if it's something you do to … cope?"

"Cope?"

"With … I don't know … being afraid?"

I give it as much thought as I can. "I *am* afraid," I admit, "of letting her down. I'm not a strong person, Joan. You would have been a much better choice for her to go to the meetings with."

"You're going to be great." She gestures at the books. "I wouldn't bother to read them. Helen will love knowing that you got them. That's all." She sits on the sofa and kicks off her shoes. "Life sure is upside down and sideways right now."

I sit next to her. "It is."

"On top of this, my *dear* husband won't let me start my wonderful, new business."

"New business?"

"My buns."

"Are you serious? That's fantastic! The business part, I mean. Tell me!"

She shrugs unhappily. "Not much to tell. I made some for Roger, and I told him about my idea. And he just said no."

"But … why?"

"I have no idea. He spends day after endless day away on business. So I told him I needed something to look forward to, for my second half of life. And to feel special about something. You know, like what we talked about."

"What did he say?"

"He said, 'I want you here when I come home.'"

I'm not able to hold back a grimace, but I repair it as quickly as I can and say, "Huh," in a nondescript tone.

"He's always been insecure. Maybe because of the kind of work he does. Being a divorce attorney and all. He's seen a lot of breakups over the years. And I don't want to worry him or throw it all away going after frosted buns."

"But a lot of men have no problem letting their wives start a business."

"I know, but he's … I don't know."

"He likes to be in control. Of things. Of you. If you could both lighten up on the old rules, some new ways might be good for both of you. Look at Roger. His business looks at cases, facts. So give him some. About your business. Show him how it's good for him too."

"I'll have to think about it. Because he's right. It would be a huge change. Roger hates change." Her voice turns brisk. "Anyway! You said over the phone that Helen had something for us to look at."

"Oh, right. She wants us to look at it and then, when we visit her, talk about *it*, not the surgery." I get up and fetch the small package from my coffee table, open the card she attached to it, and read these words: "Dear Chicks in Charge. I found a symbol—for us. But I'd like to know what you think when we see each other later."

I break open the seams of the wrapping and slowly unveil her photographs from their sheltered cover. "This is her debut," I say somberly. "But without her being here to do the unveiling."

"Maybe it's safer. It's a daring step for her. You know how sensitive to criticism she is," Joan says.

Together we examine the black-and-white photographs. Each is simple but tells a compelling story: a rusty gate hinge; new daffodils next to remnants of withered fall leaves; a collection of watering cans.

"These are wonderful!" Joan exclaims.

I continue reading: "The one I think of when I think of our lives as the Chicks is the nest." I hold up the one she must mean, of a small, empty bird's nest, tattered but sturdy, with a soft cushion of fluff in the center. On its edge is a bird, a common thrush, captured in perfect black-and-white shading, poised, ready to take off. There's a sense of completion. The nest at its feet has been a place of safety, the edge a place where each fledgling hopped before trying its wings for the first time. A moment of endings and beginnings. "It is like our lives."

We stare in admiration, then I go back to her note: "I'm teaching myself to be still and wait. I look for how the light moves. And it was as if the bird understood and waited for me to take its picture. I'm working on capturing the story in the eyes. That's where the beauty says it all."

"So true," Joan murmurs.

"I love photography so much that who I am behind the lens tells me a lot about who *I am*. The same for the Chicks. What you love, and what you do, is the story of who you are. With friendship always, Helen."

We each retreat to our thoughts about the photographs. That she was thinking of us with such love while having to prepare herself for surgery … Was she feeling optimistic, or was she scared and wanted to make sure we saw her photographs in case of a different outcome? And that she trusted us enough to show us not just photos but something more inside her.

"I need to think about my story," Joan announces. "I need to look at what I do and love. Whom I love."

"You'll have our support. You know that, right?"

She nods. "I'm counting on it."

Time for a Lift

I DIAL THE KNOBS that update the gauges. Jotting down the details from the automated weather voice on ATIS [Automatic Terminal Information Service], I predict the runway in use that favors the wind. Yes—runway in use: 19.

Love that runway. My first one, with Will.

"Current with Charlie. Will get Oakland's ATIS when out 10 miles," I announce. "Charlie" is the latest broadcast of conditions relevant to my airfield.

No one named Charlie is seated next to me in my airplane, though I'm sure I'd prefer him to the one who is, as the voice to my right commands, "Load PA [pressure altitude]. Tell me what the DA [density altitude] is and runway distance needed. *Before* taxiing." The captain seems particularly peevish today. "Time is 1651 Zulu."

"Then, Captain, Charlie's about done. In a couple more minutes, new weather data comes ..."

"Do it," he says, as he keeps an eye on his wristwatch. Timing me? Or maybe counting down until this lesson is over. Or both.

"Based on Charlie, we have the following air density and takeoff roll of ..." I begin after looking over the charts in my manual.

He checks his watch. "Nope. Charlie's done. Get on Delta."

"The airline?" I quip, grinning. He remains fixed on the front windshield. I recalculate.

The language up here is short and fast, spoken in abbreviations and acronyms that convey a story of motion but not the entire story. The tower,

81

a voice in my headset, decides what part of it I need to know. The entire story is never told. I am curious to know the missing details, which irritates the captain. Often.

On the way back from Oakland, a new story unfolds.

Tower to MJ: "83Bravo, go-around! Go-around! Number two for landing One-Niner Left."

There is something not right on the airstrip, and I must abandon my landing, my wonderful set-up-just-right-for-landing approach. This brave, new world of air-speak is becoming great fun and more so all the time: listening, replaying, and putting it into action. Even if the action plan needs to change.

MJ to Tower: "83Bravo, going-around. Number two, One-Niner Left," I repeat as I throw in all the power again and reconfigure the airplane's altitude, position, power, and flaps. I muse aloud, but without relaying it to the tower, "What the heck is going *on* down there?" and take a peek out of my side window to see the airport's emergency truck driving along a taxiway.

"Who cares?" says the captain. "Doesn't matter why! Do what they say!"

"Right! Right." I watch as airplane number one begins to descend again, and then reset Bravo to land but feel it's less ideal than before. Seconds later: "Um, Captain?" *Stop! Bad idea! Don't ask!*

Grunt. "Well, what?"

"Is the tower ever—wrong? Even if I followed their direction, could I get into trouble?"

"Damn right, they can be! Stay sharp! *They* get to walk away from mistakes. Not *you*!"

That's why I want to know *why*. Bravo has so little to tell me. No radar, no warning instruments. The tower has more of the story to tell, eyes closer to the runways, eyes watching the moving spots of aircraft and shifting rain cells on the circular faces of their radar screens—things pilots are blind to.

"If I knew more, I mean, it *could* be useful …"

"Fly! No time for this—chitchat."

I once asked "why" about a go-around plot point when landing with Will, and he had said that, if they're not too busy, they don't mind telling you and to give it a try.

I did and was told that a migrating flock had settled in the middle of the runway. "You'd be bowling onto real duck pins," they'd joked.

Will and I had laughed. "Good one, tower," Will transmitted back.

The biggest step in any pilot's life is to fly solo for the first time. I thought my turn would have come by now, but the captain continues to find things to criticize: my timing to turns, my banking to the left and most times to the right, and the other day my leaving the seat belt unacceptably folded on my seat upon exiting. Until the captain gives me his nod, I'm a fledging stuck in the nest.

The captain always wears his time-honored, heavy, brown leather bomber jacket and keeps his jaw in motion by chewing gum. His gum popping is a signal he's in the area, so before he struts through the buildings to the training classrooms, he has unwittingly warned everyone from mechanics to clerks to dive into their seats. Even the airplane pictures on the wall seem to fly in opposite directions.

In the plane, I can hear the sound of him chomping gum in my headset. He chews a little faster when I fly downwind, and I am just minutes before touching down.

"I didn't hear you say your landing checklist," he declares as I start to descend to the end of the runway with a giant "32R" at its receiving end. *Chomp, chomp, chomp.*

"I checked it. Accepted clearance for landing."

"Say the list out loud! Gas, undercarriage, mixture, power, carburetor, flaps, lights. All of it!"

I'm an ever-tightening knot of second-guessing and blunders: My rollouts from turns are delayed, the altitude is overcorrected anticipating the next remark, and each time I fix things I hear his guttural growl in my headset. In between these episodes of exchanging mutual aggravations, we argue.

"Are you turning? Where the hell's the rudder in *that* turn? Don't forget the rudder!"

"Stepping on rudder."

"Step on it! Not brush it! Crab into the wind," which means to shoulder my airplane into the wind that would otherwise push Bravo off track.

"I *am* crabbing, Captain!"

"Crab more!"

I turn to look at him. *Don't tempt me.*

He barks out what the six gauges in front of me say. He had demanded that I change the method and timing of every maneuver, so all the maneuver flashcards I made during my months with Will have been reworked. I've heard there is more than one good way to pilot an airplane, but it's clear to all of us: It's the captain's way or no runway.

I especially miss the lessons with Will on sounds that are the voice of the machine: why the engine roars to climb, or drones with boredom, or sighs on descent; of how flight is endless art; of how science can make an airplane one can pilot; of how an airplane can make a pilot into a better person and make that person into a poet. Nothing like that comes out of the captain.

Sometimes I dread climbing into Bravo. Sometimes after a lesson I sit in my car and cry. *How did it get to this?* For five months I've committed endless hours to my study and practice of flight. I think of Helen's words and am crushed to confess that I've stepped away from the dream and into a nightmare.

In the hallway my classmates avoid making eye contact. They've all soloed already—weeks ago.

"How'd it go, MJ?" Tom inquires politely.

"He keeps saying in another lesson or two. What do I have to do to convince him I'm ready?"

Tom shrugs sympathetically. "He told me that as long as the tires and wings stayed on the airplane after my landings, I was ready to go."

"But my last time was a real squeaker! Rubber kissing the runway." (A pilot's favorite landing sound.) "So I say to him, 'Nice, huh?' And he says, 'What? Oh, sorry, I was looking out the window, making sure you stayed on the centerline.'"

Henry shakes his head. "Too bad. Wish you were still bringing in cookies though."

I stomp out and hear Tom say, "Shut up, Henry!"

Henry's innocent response: "What?"

Several weeks later on a gray winter morning I wake, look out the window at the high, calm clouds, and just know: This will be my day to fly solo. The captain has only grunted lately after my maneuvers, indicating that I have exceeded the standards required to get him to stop yelling. Or maybe I'm simply outlasting him.

"I might go flying alone today," I say to Jim.

He kisses me. "You'll do just fine."

Is he saying this because he thinks I *won't* do just fine? I go into the kitchen where Blake and Annie are in a heated argument about how to get packed for school. I try to breathe while pouring corn flakes. I try to remember to breathe after each breath and think of the yoga peacefulness I've learned with Helen: *Om, Om, Om.*

"You don't put the sandwich at the bottom. Not under your books!"

"It won't squish. See? This folder protects it."

"You'll have jelly oozing all over ..."

"Please!" I shout. To their startled faces I explain, "I'm going to fly the airplane today all by myself. I have to focus."

"You'll do great, Mom," Annie says sweetly.

"You've studied it a lot," adds Blake. "Just remember: Speak clearly."

The route to the airfield comes automatically. It seems so long ago that this familiar destination was once foreign, when I first took the freeway to the thoroughfare to the side roads to where an airfield, tucked away among hills and rivers like a lost horizon to a dream, awaited. Like it had always been waiting, waiting for my arrival. I park outside the classrooms. No one else has arrived yet.

The airfield is tranquil, having meditated under the stars throughout the night. The runways are silent as aisles at an empty cathedral. Early-morning fog lingers, then begins to stir and drift slowly away. Between the grey vapors come the first rays of sunlight, warming the numbers and stripes. *My runways.*

I collect my flight bag and armload of books, and throw several peppermints into the pocket of my tan jacket to have ready when I take full command in an hour. A solitary mockingbird hops to the ledge of a nearby hangar, ready to greet its first visitor. It cocks its head to me, announcing itself in a medley of staccato songs, acting like my personal air traffic controller, allowing me in but reminding me to pay attention. To everything. A thousand dots to connect. *Alone.*

Turning around to go inside, I'm surprised to see an old man. He seems to have appeared from nowhere. I look around for another car, but there's only mine. He's hunched behind the chain-link fence, staring out onto the empty airfield.

I see Bravo and grin. Not the kind of aircraft most pilots dream of but the aircraft of my dreams. It has a faded stripe and a weathered look, and I can't wait to be inside, my hands going instantly to its knobs and levers the way a devoted lover knows where to touch; when to add pressure or ease it off, as we roll and lift, climb and turn. I can almost close my eyes and feel when its roll is done and is ready to take off. Flying an airplane, once the mechanics are understood, is a unique romance.

"Nice day," says the old man, coming over to me in slow and measured steps.

"Yes," I reply. Then for some reason I add, "I plan on flying solo today. For the first time."

He nods. "Wonderful thing. Flying. I know. I learned in the war." He looks out on the runways again. "Solo, huh? Takes courage."

I want to say that my heart is fighting to get out of my chest, and my feet feel like bricks. "I'm a little nervous. A bit afraid, even." My honesty embarrasses me, and I look for his response. Maybe I'm not cut out for this. Maybe this day is really my last day.

"Good," he says. "Good for you. Don't confuse being fearless with having courage. I'll tell you something. And we young guys had to learn this the hard way. Keep your heart and head in the game. Both, you see? Your heart tells you how much you love it. But your head? It tells you to keep learning. You've got to have both to earn the love of the air. And always—I mean *always*—carry some fear with you in your flight bag." He taps my bag with his cane. "I'm not saying a lot. Just some."

"Thank you." *Where did he come from?* "Excuse me, but how …"

"Final thing: Respect it. Even a sky of blue hides surprises. Sometimes danger. It has something to teach you. Every day. Each hour you're up there. Hear me? And …"

"Yes?"

"And, if you can help it, never fly in a war. Ruins good friendships. Ruins good aircraft."

"I won't."

"Good luck. Go up. Discover it." He takes a few steps toward the hangars, then turns back. "You'll do fine. You have the eyes. Pilot eyes." His are blue like mine. Blue like the sky.

I watch him walk away as the air fills again with mockingbird calls and the colors of dawn, breaking through clouds and rising above the hangars. I envision when this old pilot was young and feel the wonder he once had in his airplane as it soared above a world at war.

I go inside, and soon after the captain arrives.

Striding down the hallway he stops and, clasping his hands behind his back, looks up at the taxidermy fish on the wall. I hear him say, "How about making this a special day?" and wait, puzzled, for the fish to reply.

"You!" barks the captain, turning to me. "I'm talking to *you*. Get your gear. Let's go."

"Yes, Captain."

He marches out, and I'm right behind him.

"Hop in," the captain says. "I want to take a couple of practice circuits around the field. A warm-up. Just another day."

"Okay." My runway favors the breeze, blowing gently over my wings as I rise. The captain hasn't uttered the word "solo" yet. *Just another day? No! Today's my day. Say it!*

"Pull over. On that taxiway," he says, as I swing the airplane back for another takeoff.

I come to a stop with the propeller still running.

He opens his door. "Keep the shiny side up," he says, the aviation version of "break a leg," then slams the door shut.

I resist the temptation to grab him and pull him back in, even though I've wanted to push him out so many times. I watch him march off, and suddenly it's just Bravo and me.

"Here we go," I mutter to Bravo. I ease off the brake too soon, and it takes a small leap; I quickly push it back in. "Hold on!" Months ago I mocked Bravo for not being airplane enough. *Am I pilot enough?*

I review the pretakeoff checklist. I take off my scarf, roll it up in a ball, and place it to the right to pretend Will is sitting there, then review the takeoff checklist. I picture the tower guys lined up at their windows to watch.

"Concord tower," I begin, then stop, release the push-to-talk button, and stare out the window at the runway that awaits me. "I can do this," I say out loud. "Right." I start again: "Concord tower, 5483Bravo. Holding short at One Right. Ready for takeoff." Then add, "Student; first solo," to let them know it's my maiden flight.

"5483Bravo. Cleared for takeoff. One Right," comes a slow and steady voice from the tower.

I repeat and line up at the end of the runway. It's less than a mile long but now looks like 10. I add power and start to roll, then faster, keeping us on the centerline until the wings are ready to break free. I gently pull back on the stick and quickly feel us lift, gaining altitude. I've popped up faster than ever because it's just me in it. No instructor. No added weight. Bravo soars. The ground falls away below, and the hangars shrink. I am alone in a moment of everlasting exhilaration, level at 1,000 feet above the ground.

"Just three times around, Bravo. We got this," I say.

Then, just as I make my first turn, I become aware of pure bliss mingled with fear. To my surprise, in the grey mist above, I feel the presence of my mother; I almost feel as if I could reach out and touch her.

"Look, Mom. I'm up here too!" I say. And I feel her pleasure in seeing me here in her realm, airborne. For a fleeting moment, we are together again.

Focus. I snap back to the moment because, like a dancer, I must take one step at a time while preparing for the next two. In this moment are many pieces: speed, heading, turning, timing, power, and fickleness of an ever-changing wind direction. *But I felt her ...*

First landing. Hundreds of feet above, says the gauge. Tens of feet. I look outside at the few remaining feet and reduce the power. I hold the wheels off and the nose up for what seems too long, letting the momentum expire, feeling it, until I finally let the tires touch. *Squeak.* Rolling. Hands and feet take their positions: rudder pedals that keep the nose down the middle, ailerons set for the wind direction, lever flaps up, carb pushed in, mixture and power full. Ready to go—and do it again. And up. I can feel the sweat rolling down the back of my shirt.

"Good job, Bravo."

We climb. Her engine hums. The tower and I keep up our exchange as they clear me for the next two orbits and landings. When I need just one more to finish, I think I'll keep it going. But the captain might not like that. So I taxi back, park the airplane, jump out, and stand there. I look at my feet, then at Bravo. I feel like I've jumped out of the Eagle and put the first footprint on the moon.

I call Jim, who is thrilled. "I knew you'd do fine," he says.

I run over to look for the old pilot who was there earlier. I want to know if he had been watching. I can't find him. He *was* there, though. I know it. We talked. He made a comment about my eyes. And the mockingbird—my favorite because of its versatile songs and confident voice—has flown away too.

89

Helen's house is filled with balloons and flowers and cards—store-bought and crayon-made.

"I'm not sure if I'm in a morgue or a florist shop," Helen jokes. She describes her surgery as "textbook," which I take to mean "no big deal for the surgeon." I'm surprised at how good she looks. Her color is good, and she doesn't seem to be in any pain. "Tell me how your solo flight went."

"Great, and technically by the book too," I answer. "Then came the scissors. That's how flight schools celebrate first solos. They cut off the tail of my shirt and wrote my name and date on it. I told them to add Bravo's full number too."

"You let them do that?"

"It's a tradition. Goes back to a time when all pilots learned in tandem-seated airplanes, the student in front and the teacher in back. When the instructor wanted the student's attention, he pulled on the student's shirttail because the airplanes then were so noisy and no one had headsets. After a first solo flight, with the instructor not there to do any tugging, the back of the shirt was removed to show the world that the student no longer needed the teacher. But that's not true. At least not for me. I still need a teacher. A *good* one. And I lost a good shirt."

"You might need a new wardrobe on the way to get this license and all its rites of passage. I can help you," says Joan. "At least you could put on a new shirt. My bad hair job is still showing," she says, pulling on a frazzled end and squinting up at it.

"The back of my shirt was so damp you could have rung it out. Anyway, I wore my 'I Love Flying' T-shirt underneath. Mom always said to go out wearing good underwear."

"And all alone," says Joan, with a shudder. "But, I mean, *look* at you! You're a midlife mom. You talk about the usual things, like stain remover for laundry. You read to little kids on library day, and you nearly burn down your kitchen every day."

I laugh. "Not every day. Every *other* day."

"What I mean is, you look so—normal. You don't fit the usual image of what a pilot looks like. A young-guy, right-stuff, fearless, swaggering sort of pilot. But there's you: doing what pilots do."

90

"I think Joan means that you're a bit of a surprise," says Helen. "A nice surprise. Isn't *that* what you mean, Joan?"

"Of course that's what I mean."

"I get looks at the airfield that say the same thing. I'm not what you expect."

"But how great!" Helen confirms. "Right?"

My mood darkens. "Should be. But flying is very male-heavy. A fraternity. Sometimes it's subtle. Then not so subtle. Like the aviation magazines on the lobby counter with buxom babes on the covers. Buxom babes—in the 21st century!"

"Well, say something about it!" says Helen.

"I have. But the guys laugh it off. Even the office staff, mostly women, just say to ignore it. It's the first time I've been in a club but not really a member of it. I've never felt that before. The odd one out. One of a minority. A real small minority."

"How small?"

"Six percent of pilots are female. I just found out."

Helen blinks. "Then all the better for you. For us. Stereotypes suck."

"I didn't set out to be different. Just wanted to fly."

Helen smiles. "Did the captain blow you a kiss as you pulled out?"

"*Please.*"

"I was worried," Joan confesses. "I've been lighting candles at church for you."

"Thank you. If it had been me, I might have burned the place down."

"Keep it up," Helen says. "In case the propeller spins off or she loses a wing or something."

"Helen. Those are not likely to …"

"You know what I mean. Whatever the likely things really are. Life has its curve balls. Be ready. As ready as you can be." Her eyes are piercing. "I get it more than you might think. We're all pilots."

"I will. Anyway, like I say, that's the technical answer. But there's something else. Something happened … a spiritual kind of thing."

"You saw God," Joan exclaims. "I *knew* it!"

"Well, not exactly. It was … I swear that my mother was up there with me. I mean, her presence was so powerful. It was like we were flying together. You know? Breathing together." I stop. Impossible to explain how *solid* she felt, exactly as if she were embracing Bravo.

"I love that you're doing this," Helen says. "Congratulations. I'm so proud of you."

"I am too," Joan says. "Forgive me if I didn't say it before. *Very* proud."

"The clock is ticking," Helen announces. "I might try taking some pictures of my children since I'll be indoors for a while. Joan, please stop pacing. Tell us what you've been doing."

"It's not flying solo, exactly … but sort of." She hesitates for a few moments, then goes on. "I've been working on a plan. For a baking business. And no, Roger doesn't know." She sits on the chair opposite the couch where Helen and I are seated. "You both are changing so much. MJ made a change. And Helen, you had a change, sort of, forced upon you. You've both grown so much in the past few months, and I've been in such a rut. I'm just standing still compared to you both. And I kept thinking about what you both have said … about me starting this bun business. And I …," she says, taking a deep breath, "… I'm going to take a break from my life. From Roger."

Whoa. Helen and I just sit and stare, then I say, "Your first solo flight too!"

"This is huge," Helen says. She tries without success to stifle a yawn. "What's your plan?"

"Never mind that now," Joan answers right away. "You just had surgery—you need to rest."

"No, I'm fine," Helen says, but she looks exhausted.

"Call me tonight if you can," I say. "I think Blake will need to go in for surgery soon."

"I will."

With my maiden solo voyage under my belt, I can fly Bravo by myself more or less anytime I want. So twice a week we take to the skies to practice over a rural area 20 miles from the airfield. I love the solitude of preparing my plane in the morning, of setting out my plans in the empty seat next to me, and of my cautious but growing confidence. My artwork isn't perfect, but the skies provide a generous canvas for trying steep turns as I swing Bravo right and left over long country roads, and slow flight when I hover, nearly as still as a kestrel hunting in the hills below. I haven't the nerve yet to try practicing stalls solo, but at the end each session, after I've secured Bravo, I promise to do it next time.

One morning, as I'm checking out Bravo, my cell phone rings.

Blake's doctor says, "I'd like you to bring him in tomorrow. I've cleared my surgical morning for him."

"Surgery … tomorrow? I thought you said we could wait a bit." Alarm squeezes my stomach. "He's at school. He's not complaining about being in any pain."

"We can't risk it. As you know, we talked about surgery even before he got hit by the soccer ball. Waiting is not a good idea. There could be other damage inside." His voice is calm, but my ears are ringing and the world has stopped. "Don't let him eat after midnight. No breakfast. I'll see you at the hospital tomorrow."

"Right. Tomorrow." We hang up.

I stand in front of a quiet, patiently waiting Bravo, replaying the call in my head as I run my finger along the leading edge of the propeller blade. *Blake will be fine. All will be well.*

Good, no nicks. I test the other blade. The airplane is ready. *I'll tell him when he gets home from school.*

The sky is so blue, fresh, and alluring …

I lock Bravo's door, pick up my flight bag, and head for my car. Heart's not into flying today. The sky will wait.

Out of the Blue

WE ARRIVE AT CHILDREN'S Hospital. Jim is with Annie and her classmates on a field trip that was planned long ago, so it's just Blake and me. Which I find terrifying, but I keep my mood light as I greet the receptionist and explain why we're there. Her smile is warm, and she tells us the orderly will show us the way.

Seating ourselves in a presurgery waiting area, I wish that Blake wasn't too old for me to hold on my lap. I would love to at least hold his hand—but that's not going to happen.

"You're going to stay right here, right? You'll wait here?"

"I'll be here the whole time," I promise, "until they take you to recovery; then I'll be there. My face is the first thing you'll see when you wake."

He nods; has already asked me this twice.

A young dad and his little boy come in. I do a double take: The father is wearing a T-shirt that says "KCCR Since 1944." KCCR? The initials of an airfield. *My* airfield. My eyes pop open. *What? Really?*

He and his little boy, who is wearing his own super-hero pajamas instead of hospital issue, sit next to us. The dad tries to occupy the boy with a toy airplane. He's whispering clearances for what the little airplane must do, which go ignored by its tiny pilot.

A few minutes pass, and I can't hold back any longer. "Excuse me. Do you work at the Buchanan Airfield in Concord?"

"I do!" he beams, giving his shirt a little tug. "I'm a new controller in the tower. Why? You work at the field too?"

"I'm a student pilot there. I fly 83Bravo."

"Wait, wait … sure, I know you! Well, I mean, I know your voice. Not too many female pilots there. I'm sure we've talked. I'm Martin."

"Hi, Martin. I'm MJ. And this is my son Blake." To Blake, I say, "Small world, huh?" and he nods.

"Sam here needs implants because of his ear infections. How about you? Or rather, your son?" asks Martin.

Blake sends me a warning glance, and I say quickly, "It's … personal. We'll be going home later today."

"Gotcha. So maybe you'll be at the airfield afterwards? Or tomorrow? I'll be there today and tomorrow. I'll clear you to fly out."

"No, I'm off for a while."

Martin's little boy lands his plane onto Blake's leg. "Cleared to land!" he says loudly.

"Hi," says Blake.

"I yuv airpwanes."

"So does my mom." Blake glances at me. "Are you sure, Mom? That you can take time away?"

"Of course. I want to. If you're going to be home, I want to be with you." I put my arm around him and give him a squeeze.

"Okay."

The nurse appears and asks, "Blake?"

I spring to my feet; Blake rises more slowly.

"See you around, Martin," I say. "Good luck with Sam."

"You too. Take it easy, Blake."

Minutes before surgery begins, I sit next to Blake's bed to give him important mom-to-son-as-patient instructions.

"Don't make the doctor laugh. Could make him slip with his knife." Blake laughs languidly. "And now is a perfect time to mumble because you're feeling kind of drunk, and you're about to close your eyes …"

After trying to fight it off for a few more seconds, he falls asleep and slowly releases my hand. The nurse tells me to wait in the room where I hear children laughing.

"I'll be right here, Blake," I say, in case he can still hear me, and move his hair away from his forehead. It takes me several more moments before I can leave. I still marvel that I am a parent, especially when I watch my children sleep. "I'll be right here."

I'm directed to a waiting room where a clown entertains some very young patients seated in their wheelchairs, all wearing colorful pajamas and slippers, and all with bald heads like the clown. They're doubled over laughing at his antics and mishaps, released for the moment from knowing where they are or why. My heart breaks into a thousand pieces. For them. For their mothers. For Helen. Laughter rises again, and their smiles and joy remind me of what courage really is.

I go to the lobby to call Jim with an update. I tell him I'm fine and ask, "How's the field trip? Are they having fun?" I listen, then tell him I'll call back when Blake is all done. I hang up, go back to my seat, and allow some tears. Lots of them.

Through my sobbing haze, I hear a commotion from the lobby—something about "Not needing any help. I can make it." Ending with "I'll find her." Someone is walking toward me, getting closer. Stands there for a minute, panting, then walks over to plop down next to me.

The most tired of friends with every reason not to be here says, "Did you think I'd let you worry all by yourself?" Helen leans over and gives me a loving shove. "I came to enjoy all this with you."

"You're wonderful," I say, sniffling my way back to composure.

"How's Blake?"

"Good. Okay. I mean, I don't know. I don't think they've started yet."

"You know, this happens to a lot of boys who were preterm babies."

"I know. Being here reminds me of his first weeks and all the emergency trips to the Boston hospitals." Old memories, and their tender scars have reopened.

"He'll be fine. How are *you* doing?"

"Helen, it's 11 years later, and I still feel guilty about his preterm thing. My fault," I blurt.

"It was *not*. It happens," she says. "Listen to yourself. You've studied this, I'm sure. Someone I know gave me the same answer when I got cancer. Wondering then if it was something I did. Remember?"

I nod. Advice is easier to give than take.

"Hey." She shifts in her chair to look closer at me. "What the hell have you done to your hair?"

"Oh, you weren't supposed to see it yet. It was going to be a surprise." My hair is a lot shorter. For her. "It's not the same as what you're going through, I know."

She opens her mouth, then closes it and looks away.

"You should have stayed home. You need the rest, Helen."

"I needed to get out." She updates me on her chemo treatments, which will go for several more weeks. "And thanks for having my girls over to your house so much ..."

We are suddenly drowned out by someone else entering the room with cheery greetings.

Joan sits next to me and pats my knee. "How's Blake?"

"Surgery just started. Thank you for coming."

My eyes go to her hair; cut very short like mine. For me, not such a big deal because I keep mine short anyway, but Joan's hair was always a source of vanity and perpetual attempts to grow it, curl it, straighten it, or color it.

"You too," Helen sighs. She shakes her head like she's exasperated but adds, "You're both the best."

Joan reaches into the bag she brought. "Helen, I saw a couple of things I thought you'd like." She pulls out a silk scarf and suede baseball hat. "What do you think?"

"Very nice, Joan. Thanks. You have good taste. *Usually*," she adds with a wink.

"How is your bun business coming along?" I ask.

"Roger found the business plan I was working on—I left the screen up when I left the room, and when I came back he had read it. He was furious."

"Oh, no. What did he say?"

"Turned into a big fight. But you know what? We would have had a big fight anyway—about something else. He said I should look into getting a good divorce lawyer. I told him I thought I married one." She shrugs. "Anyway, I've been getting some orders."

"Already?"

"Yeah, from people I know or whatever. My marketing plan needs a lot of work. And I'm trying to come up with names. Tell me what you think of these."

"Okay."

Joan shuffles through some papers and reads, "Stick-It-to-'Em. Nuts on Top. Hot but Soft."

Helen and I laugh. "Those are obscene," Helen says. "But then again, so are your buns!"

"Those are the cleaner ones. Would you like to hear the others?"

"You and your buns are going to get arrested!"

"Yeah, and I doubt Roger will want to represent me."

We laugh some more. The old Joan would not have been able to laugh about Roger.

"It'll be the taste that sells," says Helen.

"'The taste that sells ...'" Joan repeated. "I like that."

She reaches into her purse, pulls out a pen, and adds it to her list. She says she needs to figure out where to find the most bun-eating customers, and I suggest the airfield because every cookie I bring in is gone in seconds. Everyone knows the tower controllers eat as they send off and bring in the airplanes. Helen comes up with some ideas too, and then suggests that Joan go into the coffee house we go to.

We're so engaged in Joan's plans that I've forgotten where I am until Blake's surgeon suddenly appears, still in his scrubs, his mask pulled down below his chin. "Blake did great. He's headed to recovery soon."

I leap up. "Oh, *thank* you! It went okay? How is he?"

"Perfect."

"Any other issues that we didn't know about?"

"No, nothing. Come on back. Blake will be asleep for a little while longer. I'll give you the rundown."

Relieved, the Chicks cheer. I turn to hug them good-bye, then hear the doctor say, "Joan?"

"Paul!" Joan says, smiling suddenly. "I forgot you're in pediatrics now."

"Yes. Pediatrics," he echoes, looking flustered.

I raise an eyebrow and glance at Helen, as if to say, "Be sure to get the details."

She nods.

"Anyway, I can see him now, you said?"

"Yes, I'll take you over. They'll let you see him as soon as he's brought in." He coughs a little. "Well, so … nice to see you again, Joan."

"Yes. You too, Paul."

He turns, and I'm right behind him.

"What else? What do I need to know about Blake?"

"No sports for a while. He can go home, but he has to take it easy. He'll be groggy for a few days. Let him sleep all he wants."

Let him sleep? All I want to do is hold him. Sitting next to his bed, waiting for him to wake, I marvel that my baby has been on this earth for 11 years. Shutting my eyes, I replay the years from each birthday and each birthday party to now. I am hopelessly in love with my children. I am told to remember this, as they are destined to become teenagers in a few short years.

My mother used to say, "Time flies for moms."

Blake follows the doctor's orders to rest and within a couple of days is back at school. I head straight to the airfield.

"83Bravo ready to taxi, with Indigo," I call up to the tower.

"83Bravo, taxi to 32Left. Is that you, MJ?" he says all in one breath.

"Taxi 32Left, 83Bravo. Martin?"

"How's your boy?"

"Good, thanks. Yours? Sam?"

"Good. You're back too," he pauses. "All's good."

"Yeah. Roger that."

Two lives simply connected by a few words unveil our humanity and help each other through wide and ever-changing skies.

Late one night, I follow the call to visit the serenity of my sanctuary: the laundry room. The simplicity of folding and matching calms me as I think of my latest challenge.

When was the last time I took a test? College? The written test, by the FAA, will be on several subjects of pilot knowledge: aerodynamics, weather, flight instruments, navigation, charts, and the basics of the maneuvers. Then I think of Helen and her tests—blood tests, CAT scans, PET scans, and MRIs—and sigh. *Think about my blessings.*

My classmates were reluctant to meet early to study together until I suggested we turn it into a game, like *Jeopardy!* with categories and questions on cards. Standing at the whiteboard I host what soon becomes a noisy affair with the fuel team, parts department, the accountant, and a new instructor all joining in.

"Night Flight for 100!" Tom shouts, and when he gets the correct answer, applause breaks out.

Suddenly, from the doorway, a roar: "What is going *on* here?"

The others scatter like mice and dash to hangars and offices. I pick up an eraser and proceed to clear the board.

"We were preparing for the written test, Captain. I thought *Jeopardy!* would be a fun way to ..."

"Of course it was *your* idea!"

My classmates are sitting up straight with hands folded on their desks, like obedient schoolchildren waiting for the storm to pass. "To help us get ready for the test," I say again. "We met to study ..."

Captain Lee motions to the mounted sailfish, the one I thought he was talking to the other day. "Do you see that fish there?"

I nod.

"I caught a fish just like that one. It was him or me!" He lifts up his pant leg to show a gash along the inside up to his knee. "It's up there as a reminder. For me. For you. We are *in command* of *what we want.* Doing what it *takes* to get what you *want.*"

I wager the fish would disagree. Shaking my head, I look at it and sadly whisper, "It must have been so elegant," then realize the fish is not the only one who should have kept his mouth closed.

"Not the point!" says the captain.

"But … how?" I persist, as my classmates look on in horror.

"You see it there. Don't you?" he asks, and steps closer to me. "Well?"

"Yes. I see the fish. It's just that—some things are never really ours. To own, I mean. Like the wind. It's never mine. Not a trophy. Just to respect."

He mumbles something none of us can hear. "You're wallowing in sentimentality! You'd be better off to care about performance if you want to be a great pilot!"

I bite my lip. I want to slug him. Of course I care about performance. "Yes, Captain."

He rifles through some papers, like he didn't really hear me. "Got to show the FAA examiner what you're made of. Be willing to put it up there for all to see."

I have slipped into my seat with my classmates, thankful that he seems to have forgotten about the game and the way I incited delinquency throughout the flight operation.

"Take a couple of days to review your material, then I'm signing you off to take the test." His final glare is for me, and he strides out.

Sure enough, two days later the captain says, "Okay, off you go to the testing office. Give this to the examiner." He writes out his endorsement in my logbook, snaps it shut, and deals it back. As I take it and turn to go, he says, "But first … come with me."

Apprehensively, I follow him to the hangars. I keep reciting the formulas: to find course, to find the wind correction angle, density altitude. *What could it be? Is he going to quiz me? Yell at me again? Give me another pep talk about his fish?*

The hangar is like a museum where biplanes, new replicas of airplanes of the past, turbojets, and others are maintained and polished but rarely flown. Only our footsteps echo inside.

He stops in front of the nose of each and begins to tell me the details of its history and the power of its engines. As he speaks about one, he touches it with his fingertips, tapping in a loving way unseen before, perhaps a kindness that appears and is reserved only for airplanes. Then moves on to the next. He clearly understands the machines and, I suspect, feels he is best qualified to fly them.

"What did you fly in the military, Captain?" I ask, and run my hand along the propellers of these remarkable metal birds. I love them too.

He stares ahead, pulls his hands behind him, and considers this with a tightened chin before delivering his answer. "Fighters. Bombers. In several missions. Fired down many, and many times fired upon. Good years. Hard. But good."

"How about your fellow pilots? Your colleagues? Do some teach now too?"

"A few. Some went to the airlines like I did. Some had enough of flying and now keep their feet on the ground. Some *have* to keep their feet on the ground." With a short inhale and several fast nods, he finishes. "Some are underground. Some great ones." His chin is set, like a child told not to show—*what was it?*—sentimentality but taught to stand at the altar and be in control. But, in flying, control is never guaranteed. *Does he think his fallen brethren did not keep their eye on the goal?* Like the old pilot told me, war and flying are a perilous mix.

"I'm sorry," I say. "Were they …"

But, before I can ask any more questions, he stops, looks at his watch, and says briskly, "Time to go."

"Yes, and thank you for …" *What was this?* "… your tour."

As I walk out and look back, he's still standing there, hands held behind his back, in the company of his beloved airplanes and his memories. For the first time, I feel sorry for him.

The FAA testing office is down the street from the flight school in the shadow of the looming control tower. Before approaching the front desk, I go to the ladies' room twice.

Each testing candidate knows they will enter as a subject of suspicion and be treated as an imposter. Once a leery FAA desk officer is convinced, though disappointed, to find out that I really am who my documents say I am, arrangements are made for the test I will take—a task that takes several more calls to confirm.

I am shuffled inside a small, windowless room. My pockets are emptied, and my calculator's batteries have been removed and replaced in case a hidden problem was set or an answer was inside it. Fresh navigation charts are handed to me. Blank paper and new pencils are provided for computations or, in the case of conceding defeat, to fold into a paper airplane with an SOS, begging the proctor to let me out. The proctor stands by and cracks open the door now and then, looking to catch dishonesty, even though he tells you it's to provide fresh air.

I have to go to the bathroom again but would have to go through the entire screening process once more; I decide to hold it.

I finish the exam in less than the allotted three-hour time. I wait while my test is received, worksheets shredded, and answers corrected. My score is exhilarating. But since the FAA examiner who hands it to me seems to be in no mood to celebrate, I keep a lid on my enthusiasm.

The other scores are coming in, and I peek over the counter to see them. Mine outperforms those of my younger classmates, but they didn't go crazy studying for it, or bemoan endlessly to their spouse about how difficult it will be. In any event, it's one small step for a woman, one giant leap for women in laundry rooms pairing socks. I leave the testing center whistling and discover that the airfield is hosting some kind of event.

"What's going on?" I ask a woman, who is watching with great interest.

"It's a program to introduce the wonders of flight to kids. There's some group here called the Ladies of the Sky."

"Oh!" The history of this group—a Ninety-Nine's flying club from several airfields around California—is named for one of the first female flying clubs organized by Amelia Earhart and a handful of contemporaries. There were 99 eligible women pilots then, hence the club's name. Outside, on the ramps near the runways, a bunch of female pilots share stories and offer to give children a chance to fly in their small airplanes. Some are in uniform on their way to work for an airline, but most are chatting about their airplanes and the joy of flight.

The combination of my test score and the chance to meet some of these accomplished female flyers make me giddy. I'm sure most have been flying for a long time, and I'm also sure my inexperience will show, so I hesitate.

From behind, a voice booms, "Hi! Want to introduce your kids to flight? It's really great for them to experience!"

I turn and look into the eyes of a pleasant-looking woman in her mid-50s. Her name tag says, "Hi. I'm Marge!"

"I'm a student pilot," I explain.

Marge's face lights up. "Terrific! How far into it are you?"

"First solo. Just now finished the written test."

"Solo. Test over and, of course, charmed by FAA hospitality. Good! And?" she asks. "How'd you do?"

"Pretty well."

"Come on. *How* well?"

"95."

"No way! That's better than any score I ever got from the FAA." She turns to the rest and hollers, "Hey, everyone. Look here! A student pilot!" I try to hush her, but she's into it. "And just nailed her written!"

You would've thought I'd just returned from a mission to Mars.

Congratulations ring out, and several of them wave. "Always great to meet another woman flyer," one says happily.

We approach two already engaged in lively conversation. "'Well,' said the tower, 'you've arrived!' That was about the worst landing I've had in a long while!" says one pilot to another.

"Ha! At least not since the one before that!" chides the second one.

Marge introduces me, and they say how happy they are that I'm learning. No one here asks why I want to learn.

"One day I hope to be as competent as the two of you," I say, genuinely in awe of these flying gals.

They stop chuckling and look at me. "Competent? Oh, no. I'm not competent at all," says the first woman, who had just scoffed about her landing. "Learning all the time."

"What do you mean you're not competent? Of *course* you are," says the second woman, this time coming to her friend's defense.

"No, I'm not. And you're not competent either or you'd *know* I'm not!"

Both women burst out laughing again, a perfect audition for a flying comedy act. They have lots of stories, each more enjoyable than the last. They talk about how flying is a lifetime of learning and speak excitedly of their own recently achieved major milestones: a cross-continental flight, a promotion to first officer at a major airline, the completion of additional flying credentials—not bragging; just sharing the passion of it.

Promising to keep in touch, I bid them farewell and return to my other life, which includes a trip to the supermarket.

"MJ!" I hear a kind of reprimanding voice and turn around. To my dismay, it's Fran—the one who assumes I will soon be killed in a plane crash.

"Hi, Fran."

We exchange the usual pleasantries as her eyes examine me from head to toe. Finally, she says, "Are you pregnant? You're glowing."

"What? No!"

"What is it then? It's not that new hairstyle."

"New lipstick," I say. "Great talking to you, but I've got to dash. You know, children waiting."

If flying has taught me anything, it's to avoid—when possible—turbulence and foul weather.

I'm delighted that Helen has the energy to come out to the bar with me again. The guitarist plays the hits of our rock and roll days as before, his fingers moving effortlessly along the strings. The music takes me back, but being with Helen keeps me planted in the present.

"How's your solo flying? Still liking it?"

"Exciting. But, well, I have to admit, to be up there, with all the things that could go wrong …"

"That's probably normal. Don't you think?"

"No one else seems to talk about it."

"Do you talk to them about it?"

"Well … no. I just study and prepare each time. To keep the dragons away—or at least manageable."

"Well, there you go."

"Except I'd like to keep Captain Dragon away."

The waitress arrives with our wine. At the sight of Helen's scarf-wrapped baldness, she smiles tenderly. "Let me know if you need anything else."

"We will." Helen watches her leave, then says, "My dragon really changed. From being afraid that I wasn't living my life to being afraid that I won't get a chance to live it." She sips. "Solo flights for me too. I mean, I know I have family and friends—especially the Chicks—all around me. But still, so alone. I feel betrayed by my body; not connected. Separate from it. Like two of me at war. Thanks for going to that group with me though, MJ. I think it helped."

"It must make you feel less like you're the only one going through this."

"Right. Will you take me to another one tomorrow? And stay there with me?"

"Of course."

The support group is composed of a few postsurgery cancer patients and Mark, the leader. The members are in various stages of treatment regimens. They look at peace. I am rocking a bit in a seat not made for rocking.

Mark, a seminary student with plans to become a priest, says, "Let's open up to comments. Who wants to go first?"

A middle-aged man sitting next to me raises his hand timidly, and when Mark nods, says, "I'm having trouble understanding what I did wrong. I was leading such a clean life. Ate well, worked out a lot. I'm like the last person you'd expect to get … this."

The others murmur in agreement. "You don't see it coming," another man says. "You just *don't*. All I had was this cough that wouldn't go away. Otherwise, I felt fine. And I never smoked a day in my life."

I can tell these are the thoughts that have been going through their minds since their diagnoses. They have probably uttered these words hundreds of times.

"And how about you?" Mark asks. I wait for Helen's response, and then Mark adds, "I mean you, MJ."

Startled, I look up. "Oh! I'm here with Helen," and gesture her way.

"But how do *you* feel?"

"This isn't about me," I insist. "I'm just here to—"

"But it is. You're *here*."

"Oh. Well." I look at the group. From face to face, then at the floor, and something starts from down deep. I rub my neck and sit up straight. *These aren't just faceless people. Why is he doing this? I didn't plan on this. Damn it. Damn it!* "Alright then." *He asked for it.* "I came here to be a friend. To someone who deserves to have her life back. She's afraid. And yes. I'm afraid too. So sure. I'll tell you how I feel. This shouldn't be happening. Not to her. Not to you. Or you. Or you! This sucks!" I tell them. "And for everyone else who's ever had this," I say without elaborating. *My parents.*

"Go on."

"You're all so good. You didn't ask for this. It's so … unjust," I say, failing in my promise to myself to not be upset. When I hear some of the women sniffling, I want to run out in shame.

"We're here to talk about pain," a young woman who has lost both breasts says gently. "You should let yours out."

"This isn't about me," I say again.

"Just talk," another man says, and chuckles. "We've all shared our stories a hundred times."

I blurt it all out at once. "I miss my mother like crazy. I think I will see her again when I fly, and in fact I talk to her sometimes when I'm up there and alone. She didn't deserve it either. Didn't ask for it. She was so …" I pause, then say, "… wonderful."

"And your father?" Mark asks. "How about him?"

"Not living."

"Do you talk to him too? When flying?"

"No. Not there. I wish I could say that I do, Mark. But I can't. He was so angry. When he drank, he got angrier. When he hit ... it was worse."

"That's a terrible thing," Mark says, and puts his hand on my shoulder. "But our experiences are not us. We are not what life throws at us. We are what we do with it."

"I can't get angry cursing the storm," says the first man. "I look for peace, not perfect. Just keep calm. No matter how much you plan, the imperfect's just around the bend."

I nod. Helen passes me a tissue. "We're all learning not to expect perfect. And to not be angry at imperfect."

I blow my nose. *Okay. I will look for peace, not perfect.*

The captain's plan for our next lesson is to show him landing approaches for urgent circumstances, like what to do if the engine goes out, or if the runway is so icy or wet it will make the wheels slide, or if a landing is needed and there's no airfield to land on.

But something else is challenging me today that I thought I would have shaken by now. I was a patient several days ago for an outpatient procedure to repair leg vein damage. It's been a long time coming, a result of my pregnancies and the weight I carried. All the instructions for medications were carefully followed and ended days ago. But I don't feel right. The local anesthesia should have worn off by now.

Captain Lee climbs in, chomping gum, and then a cloud of vapor rolls into my eyes and nose. *What the ... aftershave? Coming from him? Did he spill it?* It's so strong that I need to open my window.

"Your responses are too slow!" yells the captain, soon into our flight. "Are you *listening* to me?"

Maybe I should have taken a few more days before operating heavy machinery. I'm choking on the cologne from his side of the cockpit.

"I'm trying," I gasp.

My head feels light, numb even. The maneuvers are ones I know but are now too difficult. I bring Bravo in for what is supposed to be a soft-

109

field approach and land her with a jolt. Taxiing to the ramp, we are silent, but I can feel his rage.

I cut the engine and sit there, letting the sunlight fill my face with the only warmth I feel. I can't wait for him to get out. I hear him unbuckle his belts. *Get out. Just leave me alone.*

Then, he leans back into the cockpit. To my shock, he plants a fast kiss on me. Stunned, I freeze, then try pushing him away, but I'm still strapped into my seat, anchored by my harness. He leaps out, throws the door closed behind him, and marches off.

"Son of a bitch!" I say out loud.

I shove the stick right and left, making Bravo rock back and forth. I stay inside the plane for a while to try to sort out this outrage, taking solace inside my flying machine. His fumes beginning to evaporate, I detect a trace of familiar leather and a hint of chocolate, and inhale deeply before getting out. *How dare he spoil Bravo with his fumes!*

I pull open the door to the flight school so hard that it rushes back behind me and hits the stops with a bang. I take one step into the building and stand there.

He turns his now stern gaze on me. "If you can't follow directions, how can I teach you?" he bellows loud enough for everyone else to hear.

I should expose him, but I don't know what to say. The room is filled with guys. So I just stand there seething, feeling rage and humiliation. As soon as he disappears down the hall, I search for Jan, the only other female in the flight operation and administrator of the front desk and students' schedules.

"Hi, MJ. How are you ... *whoa!* What's wrong?"

I'm shaking with fury and shock and holding back tears. "Don't sign me up for another class. I can't do this anymore."

Somehow she knows what it is. "Don't you dare let him make you quit," she says. "You've come so far. Broken into their club. Don't give up what you've worked so hard for." She opens the scheduling book and jots some notes on a piece of paper. "Here. Take this. It's the name of the new instructor who just started. He's good. You get him next time."

I take her note and, without looking at it, stuff it in my pocket. Then I pick up my flight bag and walk out without another word.

Caution—Wake Turbulence

"I *HATE* HIM!" I announce to Helen.

She is too tired to leave the house, so we are sitting at her kitchen table. I can't stop looking out the window at the perfect-for-flying morning sky.

"What did he do? Did he say you weren't good or ..."

I shake my head. To complain to her was not my plan. My plan was to come over, cheer her up, distract her, and not worry her with my little stupid stuff. "He kissed me."

"What?"

I tell her what happened: how angry I was, then stunned when he shouted at me, and that I didn't stand up to him.

"Report him! Get rid of him," says Helen, her eyes flaming. "You *must* get rid of him!"

"It's not just that. I'd have to get a new instructor, again, and start all over. It's better to just end it."

"Easier. Not better," she announces with a resolution that surprises me. "I will not let you quit. Not when you've finally found your wow."

"Maybe this is the wrong wow. Maybe there's another wow."

"There's *not* another wow! MJ, you said you were going to love it, and you *do*. That's why you can't quit." Her voice softens. "You should see yourself after you fly. It's a glow I can't describe. When I see it, I want to take a picture of you. Because when you fly, I fly."

I know the feeling; I always feel it. I sigh. I knew she'd try to talk me out of it, but I didn't expect to feel so ... obligated.

"That self-serving son of a bitch." She's back to a stronger voice. "You have to get a new instructor."

"I can't just keep getting new ones. It's time to admit that I'm just not good enough."

"Stop it. You are too. How about that group of flying females you met? Ask them if they know an instructor, another woman instructor."

For some reason, this never occurred to me. "Hey, maybe that's it."

"Do it."

That night, after I finish reading to Blake and Annie and they go to bed, I sit by myself for a while and think about Bravo, quietly waiting in the dark for my return. My little airplane that smells of leather, fuel, and chocolate. No, not *mine*. The new place will have planes that will be just fine. They're all basically the same—an airplane's an airplane. And, in the company of a female instructor and in a similar model, I'll be fine.

Marge from the Ninety-Nines says she knows someone but doesn't know her well. "Her name is Peg. Here's her number. Call her. Ask for some references too."

"Thanks, Marge. I'll do it right now." I hang up with her, call the other airfield, and set up an appointment with Peg.

"Let me see the progress in your logbook," Peg says.

I hand it to her—the autobiography of my flights—listing all the times Bravo and I went up, what I learned and when, and the sign-offs from my other instructors. I hope she's not going to ask why I'm changing instructors, but I'm prepared with "We have schedule conflicts" or "I'd like to continue, but the airplanes aren't available." That should satisfy it.

She pours over the pages, then snaps it shut and pushes it back to me. "I want you out here and up each day, every day."

"Well, I found that what works for me is to work on it every day, like you say, but with two days a week in the airplane and the others for ground classes," I say, "while my children are at school. I study almost every evening too."

"I see. Kids." She exhales with a long hiss. "Begin by doing the preflight. I'll tell you what I think of what you've learned when I see it. I'll meet you out there in a few minutes."

I walk up to my new set of wings with the tail number ending in T for Tango. It's bigger than Bravo, a model size larger with four seats, two in the front and two in the back. But the back seats are strewn with bottles of aviation oil and manuals that need to be organized; I'll do that another day. Tango has more rust in the spars and other attachment points than any airplane I've seen, but the paperwork says the mechanic has it up to date on inspections, and more are due soon. Tango's not just old, like Bravo; it's beaten up, like no one's cared about it in a long time. I take its faded checklist, wondering if I want to (or if I should) fly this old girl.

Peg walks up and glances inside. "Where do you leave the key during preflight?"

"The key? I always keep it in my—"

"It's *always* on the top panel!"

"Oh … okay." I slip it out of the left front pocket of my jeans and place it on the panel. I return to finish my inspection of this machine. Everything moans on Tango—wing flaps, ailerons, elevators—and the inside has a dusty, sour smell. This craft has nothing in common with Bravo. I feel unfaithful. This is like dating someone else when you haven't broken up with the one you truly love—or once loved.

"Ready?" Peg asks impatiently. "Let's get going. I want to see what you know. We have a lot to cover."

Is she just in a bad mood today? Is this about me, or is this her regular disposition? I call the tower, taxi out, and take off.

"Why has it taken you so long to make progress?" she asks. "You should be doing your cross-country flights by now."

I don't answer since I don't think she'd like anything I'd say. Instead, I listen to her barrage of criticisms. My clearing turns are inadequately executed, according to the way she does them. As I bank in both directions to look for air traffic before demonstrating my maneuvers, she says, "You take too long. You're wasting fuel."

I try to stay focused, but I'm feeling like an imposter up here—incapable, unworthy. Soon I get a sense of this aircraft. Although it's like Bravo, it handles differently—the throttle needs more pull, the flaps feel slow—and conveys its quirks, while Peg next to me continues to look glum.

I call out the steps to hover and show her my slow flight example, usually my favorite, then increase the power to cruise along. "How's that?"

"Needs work. Put it into a stall and recover."

"In a stall? But I need to know—"

"You do know *stalls*, right?"

"Yes, but—"

"Then let's go."

I break into a sweat. The steps should be almost like the ones for Bravo, with a few changes like extra power, and I look at the airspeed indicator for Tango. *Just do the rest of the steps.* I've memorized them to keep the dragons down, to keep them small.

"Power off stall," I announce. I pull up the nose of Tango and count to myself *one-two-three*, then take away the power slowly. Too fast could make for more engine problems, especially for this old machine.

"Keep going!" shouts Peg.

I say every step out loud: "Power back, mixture in, carb heat, flaps ..." until the airplane exceeds its angle of attack to the wind and drops down as it breaks from lack of airflow. I catch it and firmly keep on the rudders, bringing it back to a working airplane. "There you are!" I say, feeling relieved and amazed. "Not too bad."

"Not too bad?" Peg smirks. "You need to speed it up. Too big a drop! I'll need to show you the right ways." Then suddenly she screeches, "Oh, God! Oh, God! What's *that?*"

Now what have I done? I look out the window, expecting to see that I am heading directly at another airplane.

"Bee!" she shouts, pointing, and I see our hitchhiking cabin mate buzzing as it bounces against the windshield. "Kill it! I'll take the airplane!" She takes over and throws a navigation chart at me to use as a fly swatter. "I'm allergic! You have to kill it before it stings me!"

I start swatting at it, and it drops to the gauges, then flies back up to the windshield, mad now.

"*Kill* it!" she shouts again.

I can hear her in my headset breathing strongly. I picture her being stung and having a reaction. I picture her having a heart attack from rage or panic, slumping onto the stick and sending Tango into a dive. I picture having to land this quirky craft on my own. Of all the study cards I've made and studied about what to do in the air in case of emergency, bee swatting is not among them. *Get the bee. Get the bee.* I keep flailing with the chart, but the bee flies into the back of the airplane.

"*Goddamn* it! Get it!"

I unbuckle—an FAA no-no—and take off my headset, and instantly Tango's inside world bursts into a screaming roar. I turn to see the bee on the back window. Meanwhile, I hear Peg call to the control tower that we need an urgent land, that a bee in the cabin is a hazard.

I can't hear the tower, which has probably cleared us right away to land.

Peg says, "No, not a medical emergency. Not yet."

Yes it is! This lady is crazy!

I continue to thrash at the windows; then, pushing aside oil bottles, crawl into the back compartment where it's even grimier than it looked. Trying to avoid some black gunk on the seat, I at last smack the bee hard, and it drops.

"Yes! *Got* him!" I shout, giving him a few more smacks. Clambering back to my seat, I buckle up. Breathless, I pull on my headset.

Peg's colleague, a fellow instructor, is in another airplane not far from us. He has heard her call to the tower and pipes in on his mic, "Oh, Peg!" he croons. "Why don't you just let it sting you and put you out of your misery?"

"Shut up, Wallace!" she snaps back at him, then offline mutters, "Jackass."

I don't dare move or even breathe, just stare out the window and wonder how she's flown for so long. *What if I hadn't been here to kill the bee?*

Moments later we approach the field to land. She clears her throat. "Like to try to land it?" she offers in a high voice that has suddenly changed to charming, like that of a hostess proudly offering her guest a tray of fine hors d'oeuvres.

I blink in disbelief. "Uh, no, thank you. I'd rather just watch you. Watch the *right* procedure first." She shrugs and brings us down. Once on the ground, I see drops on the windshield. I swipe them with a fingertip and rub them with my thumb. "Oil?" I ask in disbelief, "coming from the propeller housing?"

"It's fine."

"But I've read where a propeller can seize from lack of oil." *Something far worse for all than a loose bee.*

"It's fine. That plane can still go up again before it needs maintenance." Without another word, she heads back inside, leaving me to rest for a moment against a broken airplane.

A pilot can feel the soul of an airplane. This weary and sad airplane probably invited the bee in. I wipe a drop of oil, like a teardrop, from the nose cone of the propeller.

"Nice try," I whisper, and then, "Good-bye, Tango."

Grabbing my flight bag, and not even bothering to get Peg's endorsement for the lesson, I go in search of Tango's mechanic. After I explain the situation to him, and he agrees to service the airplane, I drive back to my flight school in Concord and make an appointment with a new instructor named Kevin.

Kevin is young and quiet, and tells me that he and his wife are expecting their first child in a few months. I explain that I plan, after his instruction and approval, to take the final test for this intended first—and only—license. And hope to do so before the baby arrives.

"Deal," he says, and we shake hands. I'm back to 83Bravo.

When I tell Helen about Peg, she says, "You were flying with the Wicked Witch of the West! I bet she usually teaches on a broom!"

I still can't laugh. "She tore my confidence to pieces."

"Maybe she was threatened by you. Maybe she's insecure and didn't want to share the sky with you."

"But she's the one with the credentials. The years of flying!"

"She has dragons too," Helen says in her wise way, "that she put on you."

"It was my fault. I should have checked her out first. Oh, that reminds me. I have something for you." I pull out a little box wrapped in pink ribbons.

She opens it and laughs. "A hot-pink Speedo!"

"When treatments are a thing of the past. Maybe you'll rejoin your swim class?"

"Maybe. Now all I need is a new chest. And I should be ready to wear it by summer."

"You'll look great." Then, looking around, I ask, "How's your home-improvement thing going?"

"Keeps me distracted. Brad thinks it's good for me. I'm doing it for him. Now the painter needs me to decide on a color for the living room." She points to several paint colors that have been rolled out in arches on her living room walls. "What do you think?"

"That one's sad," I say. "Too deep. Too green."

"And that one's the color of the doctor's office."

"Out," we say together.

Then Helen says, "I'm going to need hormone replacement too. Just got some samples to try soon. Maybe you know something about it. A vaginal ring?"

"I don't know anything about them. How do you ... with ... a ring?"

"I was sort of hoping you'd know."

"How would I ..."

"Let me call him and ask." She pulls out her cell phone, making the call with a single punch of a button; a frequently called number. "Hi, this is Helen. We spoke earlier ... Fine, thank you. I have a question about using the ... Yes, I looked at the samples ... Do I like any of them? I haven't really *used* one yet ... First I need to understand how to *use* ..." She glances at me, shakes her head, and says, annoyed, "Well, because a vaginal ring is a new thing for me, and I don't know ... a vaginal ring ... Oh. Right ...

119

You'll come by tomorrow? That will be fine then. Thank you." She snaps the phone shut and tosses it across the sofa. *"Crap."*

"What?"

"That was the painter!"

A week later, on a fresh morning with the winds light and variable, I walk out to the ramp and over to my airplane. I have several dozen more hours of practice and instruction to put in my logbook before taking my final flight exams.

Stories fly around the flight school about this examiner—a sort of wizard of the air—who can almost sense his way through the sky and sum up in a moment the character of the pilot in his presence. Once, a cocky student pilot believed he had found a runway to circle above, so the examiner let him keep circling until he realized what he had found was no runway at all—just the faint letter "I" in "CALIFORNIA" in the body of the navigation chart. He failed.

After my flight lessons, after I turn off everything and secure Bravo, I jump back inside and pretend to fly it all again. To correct the mistakes: *Not that switch; the other.* To improve my calls to the tower: "Concord Tower, 5483Bravo ..." *Not over.* "... Abeam." And use the stick and rudder roll in together, then kick it out. All because I want to be Bravo's flight specialist and know how she works and why. Not just use her switches and knobs.

And I've started to take my studying deeper, finding out about the relationships: Why do low-pressure systems turn to the left and high-pressure systems turn the other way? Why does that affect the airplane's air pressure and altitude? What is peculiar to each airfield I plan to land on and why? If one gauge fails, why is the other its substitute? Why do I still love all this maddening pile of work? *Why?* But this is more than planning for a test. It is my dragon dagger, keeping me safer. More or less safer. Never risk-free or guaranteed safe.

Since my first solo demonstrations, I have been encouraged to take short excursions. Today I plan to practice some maneuvers, take a round trip to another small airport in Modesto, and return to Concord. Inside my flight bag are the note cards I spent many hours drawing up, with all the details: what configurations the airplane will need and when; what frequencies to call, when, and to whom; exactly how to approach the distant airfield I will visit solo for the first time. In other words, completely prepared for anything.

My journeys to the air are exhilarating, and though the days may look the same, they never are. Breezes change direction and speed; clouds appear at multiple levels above and throw wind current down; the colors on the hills change as the seasons pass, from shades of khaki to soft greens.

I polish Bravo's front windshield before going up to practice steep banks. The last time our turnout was within a few degrees and almost level, changing altitude by just a handful of feet. Then we did some turns along a road and improved on some rollouts too. Still working on turns for an emergency landing. Still not ready to practice stalls on my own.

Usually after a couple or more hours in the air, I come down and make the tires spin to life again along the runway, which, like a long doormat, welcomes me back to Earth. But returning is always a bittersweet moment since my heart stays aloft, reluctant to leave the sky where it lingers for hours.

Every experience starts and stops with Bravo's key at her door, like unlocking the cover of a book, ready to savor a new chapter. Then, at the end of it, register it in my logbook, like making a brief book report.

Today's experience is about to begin. I open the door and am greeted by the familiar fragrances of the interior. All the instruments are in good working order as is the exterior. I place all my charts, extra notes, and reminders on the seat next to me. Expecting a warm day and a full list of practice maneuvers, I open wide some air vents and allow the windows to remain partly open too. Within minutes, I'll taxi to take off and begin my solo adventure. Everything is in order. Every part of me is energized.

Taking off, pushing skyward, my wings gain air and altitude. I've done this many times now: taking off and feeling the rush. The day is clear. I head to a training area where a few other small aircraft like mine practice like new fledglings that turn and circle, rise and descend, all of us stretching and strengthening our wings.

I gently swing the airplane and circle to ensure the space where I'll work is free, at thousands of feet high, from other flying machines. I call into the local frequency where a radar operator can give me useful information about bigger and heavier aircraft coming and going around the busy bay. At 3,000 feet, I set my sight on the Marin headlands in the distance, its profile easy to spot and use as a heading. From that direction comes a gentle, westerly puff, leaving its signature in the rippling waters below. John Muir's "range of light"—the Sierra Nevada—is clearly visible to the east, with peaks shining from recent snows.

I've memorized most steps to most maneuvers and say them out loud as I change the power setting, fuel and air ratios, and pitch, while soaring through air and the whole world. The nose of the airplane rises and falls, making the arrows inside the gauges dance gently up and down in their dials. I listen to the throat of the engine telling me, with its baritone buzz, that power is reduced. I look left and right and check the wing and horizon: level. Working the airplane's yoke and rudder, I stay aloft in slow flight and wonder if the reduced hum and speed are noticed by anyone looking up. Then I restore the engine to its power and hear a higher hum return.

I'm getting this down fairly well, taking only occasional peeks at the note cards I've brought and organized just to be sure I don't forget anything. Then a voice from radar control on a military base calls up.

Radar Control: "83Bravo, lighter than air, two o'clock."

MJ: "Affirmative contact on that aircraft. 83Bravo." I answer that it's in my sight and feel very proud that Bravo finally moves faster than another aircraft—even if it is only a blimp.

I pull out my card on steep turns. On a day with light winds, this is a lot of fun. Of course, I wouldn't say it's perfect but getting better. Then, after a 360-degree circle at a steep angle, I get a sassy *bump* on finishing and firmly roll out of the turn. I've felt my own wake.

Will called this out for me when we were up together. Meeting my own wake—an invisible rush of wind I've created at a breathtaking speed of about 90 miles per hour—is so thrilling that I try it again. *Bump*. Do it again. *Bump*.

It's also more than a bump. It means the turn is very level; no loss or gain of altitude. I'm like a wooden spoon, stirring soup, and when I hold the spoon in place, get a push by the flow. Inside a metal bird sits a pilot, smiling with delight, playing with the air she's stirring.

I descend a few hundred feet in wide circles but far above where sheep and cattle graze, unmoving and indifferent about Bravo overhead. With enough maneuvers done for today, I head out to my destination.

It will take about 20 minutes to reach Modesto in the interior valley. Every moment is alive. I watch the soundlessness of other aircraft in the distance, rising to their assigned places; listen to the peace that is interrupted by the chatter of local towers to other pilots; look down on the lines of roads and rails and small, inner-valley towns, and compare them to where they are on my charts. It is glorious, this architecture of nature and humankind. All mine, at my feet, outside my windows. My spirits rise. The day gets warmer. I reach to adjust the air vents.

Suddenly, *SWOOSH* go my note cards. Blown away, one after another, soaring out the window or slipping out of reach into the baggage area in back. *Oh, my God!* A stream of profanity follows. Then: *Clear your head. Fly the plane. What else can I do? Fly the plane. Ask for the frequency from radar control. It's going to be okay. Don't panic. Fly the plane.* The frequency for radar is already set. I see a blimp floating blissfully along in the distance.

I sit up straighter. My hands are sweating. In a matter of minutes, I'll arrive at my destined airport. But I've taken on altitude. I'm too high. I sort out what I must do first. I'm nearing their airspace and must be cleared before I can join it.

MJ: "Radar Control, 5483Bravo with a request." *Hurry! Respond!*

Radar Control: "83Bravo. Say request."

The voice gives me some numbers I need and rapidly dial in to know how the wind is there and the runway to use, and then can talk to the tower at Modesto.

"Modesto weather, 1851Zulu …" says the recorded system, speaking in its usual slow voice. Of all times, I need it at auctioneer speed. "… You have information Uniform." *At last.* I'm on the cusp of Modesto airspace.

123

MJ: "Modesto Tower," I begin quickly, with an artificial calm. "5483Bravo, north of the field, 10 miles; request a touch-and-go. With Uniform."

They are pleasant and tell me I'm cleared to come in. That's just fine except I had my plan illustrated on my cards, including when I should have reached a stabilized altitude and distance and speed. I'm way too high at this point and am going 15 knots too fast. I spot the airfield and see the silhouettes of the guys in the tower.

"I can figure this out," I say out loud. "I can. It's just another airfield—long, black, with white numbers on each end. Visualize the entry. Picture the approach." My heart races.

I look around for other aircraft. I'm clear. I decide to break from my heading, circle out and over the tower to fix my situation, then come back in for my setup. This is highly irregular—not the kind of standard, stabilized approach that any of my books recommend. And the FAA hates nonstandard. But here it goes.

Tower: "83Bravo," says the voice, confused. "What … are you doing?"

MJ: "I'm going outbound to re-enter. 83Bravo."

I turn back in, and in losing the altitude pick up too much speed and am coming in too fast. The numbers grow larger on the runway. Bravo barely touches the wheels on the runway when I throw the power back in, reconfigure for takeoff, and go north for Concord. *Done.* We're rising again. But it wasn't how I wanted to do it. Not how I *should* have done it.

MJ: "83Bravo northbound," I blurt.

Tower: "Roger that, 83Bravo. But, uh, let us know in advance the next time you want to practice fighter-pilot landings. Best wishes," and he snaps off.

I wish it had gone better, but chewing myself out right now will not help. Learning on the job is still learning. I shake off these last few minutes that felt like hours.

I follow the route back home in reverse, guided by the rivers, roads, and rails. In the distance is my landmark: a pond that signals to me like a metallic reflector, guiding me home, where I suddenly want to be, feeling the earth solidly beneath my feet again. I've had my fill of the sky for the day. The sheep and cattle still stand where I last saw them.

"I screwed up back there," I murmur. *Like they care.*

I set up to land, knowing this airfield and all its landmarks by heart. I come down, fighting wind gusts from the west but winning the battles with a wing lowered into the wind and a punch to the rudder. *Squeak.* Lovely sound. Exhausted, I taxi and park.

Bravo stops with a shudder, exactly how I feel. I slide down in my seat, sorting out what just happened. I close my eyes and picture the cards for my flight plan, resting atop trees in central California's orchards. How easily panic can win. How it didn't, but how easily it *can.*

Feel the fear, but fly the plane. I rewrite the cards that night. And memorize the important parts. I vow to never go back to Modesto.

"You need to go back to Modesto," Kevin says a few days later. "Shake out the doubts. Do the flight again."

The same flight? Just not the same *flight. No vents.* "Only if Modesto lets me in. Maybe I'll change the sound of my voice."

He shakes his head; to him, no big deal. "See you later."

I watch him walk off, then return my attention to Bravo, checking her before my flight. I check the fuel for any water in the lines and notice that a couple of fuel drops have landed on a pair of handsome leather shoes underneath Bravo's nose.

"Oh," I say, "sorry!" and look up at their owner.

"Hi," says a smooth, deep voice, and he steps around to meet me. His white, short-sleeved shirt festooned with bold shoulder stripes signifies his captain level.

"Hello," I say, remembering that we met a few weeks earlier inside the flight school when he was at the front desk. He was very charming, very smiling, and very eager to be meeting everyone—especially every woman.

His aircraft, he points out, is the business jet parked nearby, its turbine engines still purring as they cool. After a few exchanges regarding where he had flown in from and how far I plan to fly that morning, we're amused that the difference in distance will be about 900 nautical miles but will take each aircraft the same amount of time. I wish I had his years of aviation knowledge and skill. And I'm beginning to sense that he's hoping I'm wishing for something other than his aviation knowledge and skill.

"By the way," he points to my nose. "Right there. A little oil."

I try to de-smudge myself with a clean part of my hand. "Thanks." I don't know if I wiped it off or made it worse.

"Say, I was just wondering. This is such a charming day. Don't I owe you a glass of wine?"

It's 10 o'clock in the morning. I laugh nervously. "I tell myself never to fly *and* hold a glass of wine." I turn back to checking Bravo. Suddenly the thousands of rivets on the fuselage of Bravo require inspection. *Save me, Bravo.*

"How about after you get back then?" he says, following me. "Meet me at the bar across the street. My next flight isn't until tomorrow morning."

"When I get back? That's when I've got to pick up my children from school. And start dinner." In other words, *I'm a mother.*

"Gotcha," he says, smiling less. "So, here." He points to the third finger of his left hand. A ring is there. He tips his head at my hand. "So, is that real? Is that real for you?"

I look at my rings, though also bit oily, and give them a slight spin on my finger. "Yeah," I say with a nod. "Very real. I'm lucky." I look up at him. "And yours?"

"He's the lucky one," he replies, looking a little sorry. His stripes begin to fade.

"But thanks anyway," I add. I give him credit for his brave resilience.

In the next few minutes, I enter the lobby of the flight school and hear, in a suave southern style, "Hi there! How have *you* been doing on this fine morning?" His broken heart is already mended as he greets the ladies behind the counter.

"Hon," I say to Jim the next day as he gets ready for work. "What would you say to a glass of wine?"

"What?" Jim obliges, thinking it's a joke.

"No, I mean, let's have a date when you come home tonight. Go out for a glass of wine. Want to?"

"Sure! I'll look forward to it all day."

"Me too."

Seated cozily by a fireplace, Jim orders a cabernet, and I ask for a mocha latte. As we drink, he tells me about some of his current projects. He's got an idea for a computer pen that records a voice and plays back written notes. I tell him to get on it right away as I definitely see a use for it when I fly.

"Well, fancy meeting *you* here!" booms a congenial voice.

I look up and see, of all people, Roger—Joan's husband. I look beyond him. *Is Joan here too? I don't see her.*

Jim turns in his seat and says, "Roger," extending his hand. They shake.

"How's Joan?" I ask right away.

"Fine." Roger shrugs. "Free spirits, Joan and I. She's away on some kind of retreat for the week."

"Oh." *Funny she didn't tell me that she was going away.*

"I hear you've been busy, MJ. Got a question for you." His smile twists into a sneer. "Becoming a pilot, I hear."

I nod but feel a chill. "That's right."

"Jim works such long hours. And you go out and up, flying. Doesn't that leave your kids alone too?"

I feel myself stiffen.

Jim taps my foot with his, clears his throat, and says cheerfully, "I'd like to answer that. It wasn't just MJ's decision to learn to fly. It was a family decision. The children and I are very proud of her."

Roger opens his mouth but our waitress appears before he can respond. "How is everything here? Need anything else?"

"We're fine. Anything else for you, Roger?" Jim asks in a polite tone delivered with a subtle edge.

"No, I should head out. Business trip tomorrow."

"Give Joan our best," Jim says, then turns to the waitress. "Champagne for two, please. We're celebrating!"

Dismissed, Roger walks away.

"Bully," I grumble. "Thanks for swooping in to save me."

When the champagne arrives, I raise my glass. "To being happily married."

"To being happily married," he repeats.

"The nerve of Roger," I say.

"Let go of it."

"No, but really. You should see the way he treats Joan."

"I've seen it."

We sit in silence for a few minutes—him enjoying the mellow atmosphere; me stewing. When he offers to pour me a second glass, I nod. Unusual for me, but I'm still irked.

"I'll tell you what. Joan should learn to be a pilot. She'd have plenty of opportunities."

"Opportunities?"

"Affairs."

"What do you mean?"

"The airport is crawling with men. I should tell her. If she's looking for action, all she has to do is hang out at the airfield." I hear too much champagne in my laugh and put the glass down.

"What kind of action? You mean like *action*?"

"Yeah. Like pick a pilot and take off with him."

"You actually see that going on?"

"Sure. Middle-aged, married guys looking for something quick. Gives the phrase 'layover' a new meaning."

Jim doesn't respond; seems deep in thought.

Change the subject, quick, I tell myself, but my mind is blank.

"So guys have asked you to join them for a glass of wine? Or— *something?*"

"Um …" This is not what I wanted to talk about tonight. We're usually so honest with each other. *Should I tell him?*

"MJ?"

"Well, yeah, once. At the end of a flight lesson. The captain hit on me."

"He—*what?*"

"Jim, only because I'm a woman in a man's world. It's not because I'm so irresistible or putting out a vibe or anything. It's just that being a female is enough for some guys."

"When?"

"Several weeks ago. I dropped him. I looked for another instructor. Went to a mad woman, who didn't care if she killed me as long as she didn't get stung. So came back with another guy …"

"*Another* guy?"

"Yes, a young guy who's married. But he's expecting …"

"Expecting *what*?"

"A baby! Listen to me. I can handle this. I *have* to handle this. You can trust me that I will. A lot of it is outdated aviation chauvinism. I see it and have to work around it."

He scowls and has more champagne, which he drinks angrily, not romantically. "I knew some aviation majors at college. One made off with my date one night."

"Her loss."

"But *you*? I was all in for this, for you."

"You still can be. You were great to help me out with Roger tonight. You were …"

"I'm not so sure."

"But …" *What just happened?* My hero, the man who toasted my flying carpet just minutes ago, has now pulled the rug out from under me. "You're not so sure … about what?"

"I don't know. I need time to think it over. To be sure you're safe."

"I *am* safe! You know how much I study. And practice. I won't let you down. I promise. Hey, you know, I get into a jam, I get out of them. Cards blow out. So what."

"What?"

Shut up, MJ! Why are you still talking? You are forbidden to have champagne ever again!

"Oh, it was nothing, really … just that … the other day all my cards flew out the window. I could have panicked, but I didn't. Well, I did a little, but then I was fine, and …"

"Are you *serious*? So you were flying, and you lost all your instructions?"

"Well, it's not as if I didn't know what to do."

"If you know what you're doing, why do you still need to look at your cards?"

"Because I … because they're a backup …"

"MJ, you can't do this if you're not ready!"

"I *am* ready!"

"And don't forget you have children who depend on you. And me! What if—"

"Stop!" I put up my hand. "Don't worry."

"I wasn't before! But now it feels too …"

"Too *what*?"

"Too risky. I don't know *how* I feel about it."

Our evening out concludes in silence all the way back home. The rest of the sleepless night I lie awake, thinking of the risks of flying not found in textbooks. Despite all my studying and practicing, tonight's turbulence was not in the forecast.

A week goes by. Then another. Things are up in the air with Jim and, until they stabilize, I keep grounded. To stay busy, I rededicate myself to an old friend: my appointment book. In the blocks of time once reserved for flying, I attend a couple of PTA meetings and chase after some items for a fund-raising committee.

Helen greets me with, "I'm not speaking to you," as I step inside her house for coffee. "You're here too much. Which means you're not out flying."

"Yes, I'd love coffee," I say. "Don't bother. I'll help myself." I walk into the kitchen and see Joan standing near the counter.

"I brought buns," she says.

"Thanks, Joan." I send Helen a teasing glance. "For your warm hospitality." Taking one from the plate she offers, I ask, "Hey, did you go away?"

"Yes. How did you know?"

"Jim and I ran into Roger, and he told us."

"Lucky you," she smirks.

"So," Helen says, "why aren't you at the airfield? Isn't this usually your day?"

"I'm only taking a break, Helen. To see you more often. Not quitting."

"Really. Well, tell me: How's life again back with your appointment book?"

"These buns are the *best*, Joan!"

"I thought so," says Helen. "Look me in the eyes and tell me you don't miss that little airplane and what it has turned you into."

I can't. "Blake and Annie's school, Helen. They need help, and I'm useful. You're missed too, you know."

"I'm not working this hard to get healthy so I can go back to frenzy! And neither are you. You've crossed over—to something new. Something you love. You can't turn your back on that."

"There's more to this than me," I say, feeling selfish and angry. "Jim's not on board with it anymore. Not lately. Maybe not—again."

"He's *not*? Why not?"

"I told him about the captain."

"Why?"

"I have no idea. I felt like I should be honest."

"And he got upset?"

"A little."

"Well," Helen says, "as long as you don't tell him how your cards blew all over the place. His confidence would go out the window too, and you'd be …"

I let out a long, weary sigh.

"No! You didn't tell him about that!"

I nod. "I didn't get a chance to tell him the second time to Modesto went so well."

"Oh, MJ."

"I know." I turn to Joan. "You look amazing. Happy. And you're not even wearing makeup! Tell us about the retreat."

131

"It was marvelous. We meditated. We walked in the woods. We listened to music. We danced! And three times a day we sat in a circle and just *talked*. The leader of the group asked what we did, and we went around the room and everyone said what they did for a living, you know? And then someone said, 'I live honestly.' And something in me went *ZING*."

"Wow, I love that."

"We got up at sunrise. There was no time to fuss about my looks, do my hair, or put on makeup. And you know what? It was *fun*. It was honest. No lying about my looks. No masquerades. And one of them told me I looked great. He said it like that: 'Joan, you look great.' To be told that ... by a man ..."

Helen and I stare in delight at this new Joan. All of a sudden something hits me. When I called Blake's doctor to schedule a follow-up appointment, I was told he was away for the week. *The same week.*

"Was Paul there?" I ask.

She's surprised but then grins. "Yes, he was. But it wasn't like we did anything. We connected. With each other. With everyone else there. With ourselves."

"But does that mean ..." Helen asks. "Are you ..."

"No. I'm not going to *do* anything. Except be honest. With Roger. About our marriage that stopped working a long time ago. About living a lie. No more." She takes a bite of one of her buns, swallows, and shakes her head. "My God," she says, "these buns *do* kick ass."

Flight Risks

TOO MUCH TIME OUT of the air throws my confidence to the wind. I could just go up and not tell Jim. Or make a bargain. Or stay grounded to study; there's always study. But flying is not found in a book.

I can deal with this. Of course I can. It will make me feel so much better to go to the airfield. I won't have to fly, just show up. Smell the air—sweet from refueled and ready airplanes—and hear the firing of the propellers. See how my classmates are doing. Did Tom talk to his parents yet? Do Henry and John plan to become instructors one day?

I pull in and park. My flight bag is handy. In case. I go in and greet Jan at the desk.

"Hey, stranger! I've missed you. But things at home are kind of up in the air—wish one of them was me."

Jan stands and rounds the desk until she is right in front of me. "MJ, I called you several times. But I didn't want to leave a message."

"What? Why?"

"It's about Tom."

"My classmate Tom? What about him?"

"He got into … some trouble."

"Trouble? With his parents? Did they find out?"

"No. He had an accident …" She stops midsentence, and I search her face for the rest.

"An accident. You don't mean … not an accident in the air?"

"On his motorcycle. A couple of days ago."

I step closer to her. "Jan, is he okay?" She looks down. "Jan? Where *is* he?"

"He's … he didn't survive it."

I freeze; stare at her. Had to have heard her wrong. It can't be! Then I become aware of others in the lobby. John, Kevin, the guys from the hangars. No one is speaking. No one is moving.

"No!" I put my hands to my head. "*Please,* no!" I beg. Jan reaches out and pulls me close while I sob. "He's just a boy!"

The church is jammed with mourners. When in the business of working with the departed and it's your turn, there seems to be no shortage of support—or flowers; their fragrance fills the air. The arrangement from Tom's flying friends is a model of an airplane he flew, done in small, white roses.

We soon learn that Tom's family had known about his flight lessons for a long time but pretended not to when he disappeared during the morning, to allow him time to join the sky. Jim and I sit in the company of others from the flight school. Henry and John, my fellow student pilots, wear their dashing leather jackets, and both have brought their girlfriends. Henry keeps his head down and his pilot glasses on.

The service begins, and I can hardly hear it. I weep like I haven't done for a long time, for all whom we've loved, lost, fought for, and still fight to keep. For Tom. For Helen. For life.

Tom's parents greet each of the guests. When I introduce myself and Jim, Tom's mother, who is in a daze, says to me, "Oh, yes. How are your lessons going?"

"I've been away from them for a while. But Tom was my favorite classmate. Everyone's favorite. He loved to fly. He …" I stop.

"Thank you. He loved it. We know. We knew because when he'd come back to his job—to us—he was *so* much happier," she says through tears and smiles.

I hug her, thinking how incomprehensible the loss of her child must be. The next guest steps up to quietly extend his hand, and I move to the side.

I notice that Jim is looking around. "The captain's not here," I say, to alleviate any worry he might have while I blow my nose.

He shakes his head. "No. Not that. But … you need to go back."

"To Tom's mother?"

"To your flying. You *need* it. Just be sure to … be careful."

"I will be. I have been. I'm careful and prepared and …"

He's crying too. "Otherwise, what's living for?"

Days later, after having made all the preparations, I climb to several thousand feet, alone, on my way to practice rolls and steep turns. Looking out my window I check what's below—in case I need to be there. *Know your options*. Options highlighted on a page of a text, on the page of lecture notes. I'm a book pilot with more hours behind words about flying than behind a stick, flying. But the stick gives a far better lesson.

Over an hour ago, after a thorough review of all the usual weather reports, the control tower and I exchanged the customary words of departure: "Good flight, Bravo" and "Good day, Tower. See you later," to signal our good-byes. *Superstitious*.

Now flying alone, with gauges and charts as my steady companions, I keep a pen and notebook for important details from other towers and other pilots. I am going out further than I usually do, to look at different exposures on the mountains, and then along the rivers, glistening in the hazy sunshine. Miles melt together.

I look down at farm fields and rivers running with winter rains. I think about the invisible—what I would see if I continued to the southwest for 250 miles: the beaches of southern California. And if I could go straight up for that distance, I'd be in the neighborhood of satellites. The world feels pulled together on this flight with Bravo. We are at the hub of it all. Nothing feels very far away.

I hum as usual, filling the airplane with my own pitches of music, feeling like a bird scanning the corners of the skies and looking down at the world rushing underneath. I scribble a note—"at peace"—to remind myself of this moment; of being in the air again; that everything feels within reach. But my handwriting looks like lines on a heart monitor, my pen lurching up and down each time a few fast bumps of air hit Bravo.

After finishing some attempts at steep turns and trying to maintain a wide circle, I decide to return. The bumpy air is getting stronger, making my maneuvers disappointing. The circle is pushed out and looks like a series of loops from above, and the steep turns are fighting the wind and becoming too steep, making an unintended stall possible. Strong gusts are coming over the hills and rolling down and over my airplane, dealing sharper, faster shoves at Bravo. Definitely time to go in for the day. I tighten my shoulder harness and seat belt.

I listen for the current conditions on the airfield to know the runway to use and the airspeed over it. *No information comes through.*

I check the call numbers. *Not working on their end?*

I call the control tower to request to land. *No response.*

I wiggle the headset jack, check the circuit breakers and frequencies, increase the volume, and ask again. I wait. *Nothing.*

Come to think of it, I haven't heard other pilots in the vicinity either, with their usual ricochet of words. All is silent except for the purring of the propeller. More bumps. Then harder.

"Tower, how do you hear, 83Bravo," I say. "How do you hear?" *What the* … I ask again. *Nothing.*

I re-examine the frequency. *Yes, right. Try again. Nothing again.*

Have to accept the idea that I have no operational radios. *Fly the plane. Don't panic. Think. Now what?*

"Okay, Bravo. Up. Power in, climb, circle."

My heart pounds harder. In minutes I am higher and circling, looping out and making a wide circle back to keep from being blown into the hills, still listening to the sound of trouble wrapped up in silence.

Options. Priorities. Fuel. I calculate my remaining fuel. With the wind pushing hard against me in the direction I need to fly, and since I've gone farther out and used more than I planned, I have the raw truth: 20 minutes of usable fuel remains. *Good enough. For now.*

I look at the horizon and see fog—a grey wave in the distance—rolling in. *It's not supposed to be here yet! It's not forecasted for now. Much later. It's too early!* And yet, here it is, advancing swiftly. Pilots can lose control, blinded inside such fatal folds of grey. Without radios and in impending fog, I will be flying in the blind. *Shit. Fly the plane. Weather deteriorating. I must get down. What is best?* I continue to circle, think, looking for air traffic. I am alone in the sky.

How about other airfields? I rustle open and check the chart. Using the length of my finger as the measuring tool, they're about the same distance as the one I left. Fog could be in those areas too. Or maybe not. I can't know without radios. I look outside, and my thoughts spin: I could go directly below and land on the farmer's craggy pastures. Bravo could break, wheels would snap, a wing might shear, but I could live. I have to. Even if it's Bravo's last day, it can't be mine. What if fuel starts a fire? I will run. *Shake off these thoughts. Fly the plane.*

I look down to see if I can find the flattest, cow-free place. Then I check to see if Concord is still open. Circling, I see the fog in a steady march. I need to decide if that is my best option to land. *Ten minutes.*

Suddenly everything and everyone feel very far away—and I've been expelled from the world. But I am not forgotten.

"This will *not* be my last day," I say out loud.

Bravo's propeller continues to purr along. A lonely monotone, waiting for my command.

More options. My radio emergencies card. Finally extracted from my papers, I see another option. I dial the code for an aircraft, alerting the local control towers that I'm flying in silence. A code that reaches my field and maybe a military base some miles north but ... military. Their planes get signals too! If one is passing overhead, it could get my signal and call up the tower for me and tell them to clear a runway. If one is overhead. But I don't see anything.

"Someone. Please hear this," I say aloud, and send out the invisible signal to an invisible possibility.

Rolling out, I fly west and am still out several miles from the airspace, which I'm not cleared to enter without the usual invite unless extenuating problems arise for the pilot. I fit that condition.

Another option: The tower can signal to me with lights! I look for distant signal lights, reaching for miles from their windows, telling a pilot in distress to come in. Or to stay out, if there's trouble on the runways.

"Where are your lights? Do you know I'm *here*?" I keep looking. "Come *on*. Give me a green light!"

No green to come in. No red to stay away. Maybe no one down there has received a call about me from another pilot.

Beyond the tower, south and heading north, the mass of grey is closer. Fog, charming in San Francisco love songs, is now my dragon. I make one last circle, waiting for a distant signal. *It's getting lonely up here.*

I look at my watch. I have five minutes of fuel. No lights to beam my okay to come down. *Which direction to take?* The winds kick again, and I put some power into the engine to fight the strong breezes and belting gusts, which I know will use up the remaining fuel even faster.

Will told me to watch the ever-changing directions of the wind: "Look at ripples across the ponds and the blowing field grasses."

But today there must be wind shear because wide patches of brown grasses are moving in different directions. Bravo continues to be punched by wind. *The fog. Look at the fog!* It's moving from the direction that I should land into, and that is from the south. Fog, the destroyer, now pointing the way. I scan for other aircraft. *Have they cleared the way for me?* I set up Bravo for a landing.

"Concord Tower, 83Bravo, landing, taking 19Left. No radio." Down into some slapping wind, down to the earth again, hoping there are no problems on the field. This must work, a one-shot try. No time for a go-around. That's not an option.

I make a base turn, out far enough that might make me better seen by the tower, still miles away. I will need more power to push into the wind. I will land long, deploying less flaps and going further down the runway than usual, with more speed—all to muscle against it.

My knees are shaking, and I try to ignore them as the earth rises up. I take some power out. It's sinking. Impatient, I pull back too much. Bravo sinks more. I kick in the rudder, and the wheels hit hard. Ailerons are full into the wind to taxi, and we're still feeling the gusts.

Finally, we come to a stop.

My whole body is shaking, and I say aloud, "Bravo! What was *that*? You cut me off from the whole world!" I know it's not Bravo's fault, but I'm feeling hysterical. "Don't do that *ever again*!" I give the top panel a bump with my fist. Then feel bad; not like the engine quit.

I tie down, then hurry to the mechanic's office inside the hangar.

"Hey, MJ," my favorite mechanic Steve calls out as he rubs his hands on his oily, red cloth.

"What the *hell*, Steve?"

"What?"

"The radios! In Bravo. They're out!"

"Out? Oh, shit. Sorry! They fail sometimes. I'll fix them. Were you solo?"

"Yes!"

"Sorta scary, huh?"

"Sorta? And the fog rolled in. Early."

"Can't fix the fog. But you're back. We like to see pilots come back. Good for you!"

"Well, thanks." I start to calm down. "They worked when I left. Just quit in flight. Not your fault."

"Bravo's radios will be fixed," he says. I turn to go, and he adds, "And really … good for you."

Later I learned that a military transport jet overhead had received my distress signal about my radio failure and called in for me, someone whom I'll never meet but who reminds me that flying solo doesn't mean you're all alone. My flight family—other pilots with voices that greet, guide, and squawk like members of a migrating flock—had come to my aid and called the local towers. The tower had cleared the field for Bravo to land.

Helen has invited Joan and me to look at her newly painted living room. She leads us inside where her photographs adorn the walls like a gallery of fine art, each framed with a light from above. In the center is the famous bird's nest, built to last, the mounds of purple mums letting in the one of yellow, the silence of morning dew on long leaves of grass.

"They each whisper *endurance* to me," Helen says, "in a simple form but complex condition. They each have a purpose in life; something to help them make the most of it. To keep them from retreating, from giving up."

139

"These are just amazing! Just wonderful," I say. "You have a real eye."

"A *real* eye," Joan agrees.

I do a double take at her. Gone is her glow. "Joan? Something wrong?"

"Well … Roger is having an affair."

Helen and I pretend to be shocked, but we're not; many times we have wondered about him. Once he hit on Helen. So revolting.

"Are you sure?"

"Unless I own a pair of opal earrings that I forgot about and left one in my bed, yeah."

"Oh, Joan."

She sighs; isn't devastated. "You know, Roger and I have one of those beds where you select a number for your side. To get the perfect sleep. And when I came back from my retreat, I saw that the number on my side was not my number. He said he must have changed it *by mistake*. But now I know he's been sleeping with another number." She wipes her eyes, and suddenly the storm inside her strikes. "I could have done it! I could have cheated on him! It was tempting! But I didn't. *Damn it!* I didn't."

"That son of a bitch," says Helen.

"Well, it'll be easier to kick him out. Not easy. But easi*er*."

"Will you?" asks Helen. "That's a big change. Not what you planned."

"What plans? Roger kept me in a cell. I lived by his plan, not mine."

We sit back and take it in. "He knows about divorce law," she says, conveying caution for what he will unleash. "But I know all the others who are the best too. And some of them don't like him very much. He may know his way around the law. But at a cost of losing trust. From his colleagues and their wives."

Helen smiles at this. "His day in court is coming."

"So," I ask carefully, "you seem okay. *Are* you okay?"

"I'm fine. I really am. I mean, I know I'll have my moments. But in a way, in a lot of ways, this marriage was over a long time ago." Joan smiles, but her head bobs like someone still trying to convince herself or is about to explode. "So, I'll keep you posted."

"And call if you just need to talk," I add.

"We're always here to listen," Helen nods. Then she turns to me. "How is the air up there for you?"

Ruefully, I tell them about the day the radios went out in Bravo.

"Well," Joan says, "you wanted a challenge."

"Not like that! It's the kind of thing that makes me wonder if I have the grit to do this."

"Why did you want to learn to fly then?" Helen demands. "To know all the parts? To draw the systems? You didn't just show up at an airfield one day. You had plenty of other places to show up. Like school meetings. Or shopping malls. Safe places. But you showed up at an airfield. And stayed. Why?"

So much for a tender response. *Oh, sure. You have plenty of what it takes, MJ!*

"Have you thought about why?" she asks again.

"Should have gone to the mall," I mumble.

"Do you know why?"

"I do! I went after a dream," I say, tired of the confrontation. "Is that the answer you're looking for, *Captain*?"

"Sure. You wanted to do something you love. But more. It's about the relationship the airplane brings to it all. And whether you were aware of it or not, you wanted to fly to get to know more about you—the person who had always dreamed about it."

"Why did you fly if it was foggy?" asks Joan.

"The fog came in earlier than expected. Like it was on a search-and-attack mission."

"So it surprised you."

"Of course. It came in early and ..."

"And you ignored it?"

"No! How *could* I?"

"You knew about the bad radio on the way out?"

"No, the failure happened up there. The mechanic said later that the jack was broken. What are you getting at?"

"You have to see that you played it well. Not reckless, not neglectful," says Joan.

141

Helen adds, "All that highlighting with markers paid off!"

"What if it hadn't played out so well? I promised Jim I would be safe. What if I was too late to get back? Encased in fog? Out of fuel? Out of luck?"

"Do you really think all you had was a lucky day?" Helen frowns. "Next you'll say that I was lucky to get these camera angles."

"Of course not."

"Listen," Helen says. "You looked it in the eyes and found the path down. Just the way you said it had to be done, long ago, when you told me about the poem about fear. You held it in check when the time came. Remember that day at yoga? You found a way out of the bad sky."

"It's not that simple! *You* try it!" I shout at Helen. "*You* go up where it's scary! And tell me how bad it feels to be there and wish you weren't, and think about your family and how this can't be the end of your life, but wonder ..."

Oh, wait. Oh, no! What did I just say? I put my hand to my mouth. "I didn't mean that, Helen. I'm so sorry!"

"Forget it. It's all relative," she says. "Fog? I'm sure it's a frightening sight, but so is seeing another needle going into me. No one can hear you? I'm in support groups where women say their own families don't listen to them and wouldn't know what to say if they did. You're figuring it out as you go because you weren't looking for trouble? I'm trying to figure it out too—trouble I never went looking for either."

"I am sorry I said that, Helen," I say again. "I didn't mean it. To you, of all people ..."

"Honest. It's fine. I've started doing some reading. Books on cancer. To know it better and fight it. Joan told me that you had some. So I called Jim to get the titles."

"You did?"

"Wait. You'll like this: I use highlighters too."

At last, we exhale.

"The photos are terrific, Helen," Joan says, now looking at the gallery again. "I'm going to hire you when I need a photographer for Chicks' Buns.

Come on, I brought some." Turning back to me, she says, "So, what did you tell Jim when he asked how flying was that day?"

"I told him it was a little bumpy."

An hour later Helen walks me to my car. When I open the door, she tosses a little package inside. "That's to open later. When you have a quiet minute to yourself."

The second she closes her front door, I tear off the wrap, open the box, and find a small, plush green dragon, complete with a red felt tongue and felt scales down its back. The note says, "Did you know that dragons are embraced as creators as well as destroyers? A little wisdom. And a little fear. To keep in your flight bag. Love, Helen. P.S. I got myself one too."

The next day, I return to the airfield and say to Kevin, "Can you take the stick? Your airplane."

"My airplane," he replies as required.

"Your airplane," I confirm. Then I withdraw a handful of small, gold stars—the paper kind that you lick and stick, taken from Annie's craft box. Opening my window, I hold up my hand, and the breeze snatches the stars. They trail behind us, spinning wildly before disappearing over the countryside where Tom had flown too, so many times.

"Little meteorites," I say. I bid him good-bye in silence and vow to keep trying—and flying—for as long as I live. Kevin is awaiting an explanation, so I talk to him about Tom and tell him about Tom's idea to help his family's business by taking up ashes of the dearly departed and throwing them out the window over the ocean.

"That's a great idea," says Kevin. "I think I might want that for myself someday."

I smile. "Me too."

"Okay, MJ. Time to do the maneuvers. Show me what you're made of. You have a lot to do before your final test with the FAA examiner—stall practice, long-distance solo flights, all the high-performance takeoffs and landings. Ready? Your airplane."

Hitting the High Notes

"DO IT AGAIN," Kevin says.

I've just busted my landing distance limit for a short landing by 25 feet. There's plenty of runway ahead, but the point is to bring the wheels down just past the numbers. Good training in case I need to land someday on an aircraft carrier. Or on my driveway. I keep trying, but today's short landings are over the limit. I try once more.

MJ to Tower: "83Bravo staying in the pattern."

Tower: "Number one to land."

"You almost have it," says Kevin. "Bring out the power sooner."

On my fifth try, I bust the limit again, 10 feet long. I don't even want to look at Kevin. "I'm done. I'm calling the tower to taxi in."

"I don't think I can do this," he says wearily, rubbing his palms on the knees of his pants. He started doing this on my first takeoff, and he's back to his knee-polishing again.

"But ... Kevin! I really have done these short enough before. I'm not getting them right today, but ... I mean, maybe the day is too warm? That makes an airplane float more ... but, of course, it's no excuse ..."

"Maybe," he says distractedly.

I pull off the runway, take up the flaps, bring out the mixture, and call ground control. I turn to him, feeling sick. "Do you not want to show me these anymore?"

"What?"

"My landings. You said you don't think you can do it."

"Oh, no. I'm talking about the baby. I'm going to be a father. Soon! I don't think I'm ready."

I stare and laugh with so much relief that this isn't about me. "If I can learn to become a pilot, you can learn to be a dad. It takes some practice too. You'll see. After the baby arrives, you'll get the hang of it."

"Yeah. Right."

"Trust me. You *will*."

"And what about you? You said that you'd take your tests at the time the baby was due. I'll need the OB soon. You need a date with the FAA."

"Our mutual due dates. I remember." My shoulders fall at the reminder. Five hours of aviation exams. At least that's many fewer hours than my labor experiences. *Still.* Based on the stories circulating, the examiner has failed a couple of recent candidates on their licenses.

"Study hard," he says, then chuckles. "Like I need to tell *you* that. And come out to practice these landings."

"Get some rest," I say, "before the baby comes. But *don't* study the childbirth books." Some of them are like the ones on airplane near misses and disasters, and he's already nervous enough.

The next time out, just after dawn, I greet Bravo. Her reply is a squeak of the door when I pull it open.

"The radio is all set," the mechanic promised me 10 minutes ago. "Fixed it, so you'll be fine." *Good. No more silent radios.*

I've planned several types of practice landings for today. One is to finally make a short landing short. Then I'll land, starting too high— intentionally this time—then withdraw power, tip the wing into the wind, and push down on the opposite rudder to slip toward the runway, like falling sideways. It's an exhilarating sensation, but I am told it can make your passengers scream.

Next I'll pretend the runway is snow-filled and barely let the plane touch, then do a wheelie with the nose up so it won't sink into that soft powder. I'll practice a regular landing too but pretend I need a quick escape because the runway is filled with a flock of invisible ducks and needs a controlled go-around.

Each landing takes a different type of setup. Each comes with a special takeoff too—short and soft field takeoffs. And each takes a lot of practice to get it at an acceptable level and meet all the standards. I work at it over and over, not wanting to be just satisfactory. I'm starting to feel like I'm wearing wings, not just sitting in an airplane.

Once up, I hum and comment on the beauty of the earth below and the clouds above, and belt out a few bars from "Highway to the Danger Zone." I am ready to impress myself with my maneuvers.

I am, in fact, on fire this morning and rave aloud, "Coming in. Coming in. On altitude. On speed. Good. Good."

Then, when I land it right, "*Who's* good?" I shout, "On the spot!"

Another time: "Oh, yeah! *Love* that one."

My last landing, which isn't as good, gets this response: "Well, that little sucker sucked, didn't it?"

I take off again to try some more, resuming my performance of "Highway to the Danger Zone" with enhanced gusto. All is mine today. My spirits soar. *I love this.* Then ...

Tower: "Um, 83Bravo. You'll need to make this your last landing."

MJ: "Oh. Sure. Other traffic? Something else?" *I don't see anyone else.*

Tower: "Your mic is hot."

MJ: "Say again, tower?"

Tower: "Your mic. It's hot. Stuck on *on*. It won't let other traffic call in for the runways."

MJ: "*Shiiiiiiiiit.*"

Tower: "But ... we agree ... you *were* doing quite well." There's laughter in the background.

MJ: "Sorry." I'm beyond embarrassed. "83Bravo, coming in. Full stop."

Tower (a new voice; I recognize that it's Martin): "You are such a riot, MJ. Sorry to make you stop!"

I taxi, park, disembark, and tie the wings down. "Bravo!" I hiss. "*Really?* First *no* one hears me. Then *everyone?*" Red-faced, I slink inside.

Jan in the mechanic's office grins when she sees me.

"Please don't tell me you heard about it," I warn her.

She laughs. "You're the talk of the town! The tower called to tell us. You made their day!"

"I'm moving out of state. Been nice knowing you."

"Oh, stop, silly. Even though they said your singing was awful, and your descriptions were, shall we say *colorful*. And guess what? They awarded you your new handle."

"Oh, no," I moan. "I don't want to know."

"It's cute."

"What is it?"

"*Hummer*." From the root word *hum* as in *humiliating*. Still, it could have been a lot worse.

"Hummer," I say. "Right."

Brad, Helen's husband, wants to do something special for the Chicks in Charge. Even though we tell him he doesn't have to, he goes out and buys us tickets to an Earth, Wind & Fire concert.

"It's Helen's favorite group," he says—as if we didn't know!

The only problem is that the concert is only a couple of weeks away. Hoping to preserve Helen's dwindling energy, I offer to take her kids for the weekend.

"No, I can't ask you again," she says.

"You *didn't* ask me. And I love having them. My kids love them. You'll be doing me a favor."

The last time our four children converged, Blake demonstrated his command of chemistry by setting the front yard on fire. Helen's daughters, more fascinated than impressed, had been excited about coming back.

"Please," I say. "Jim can show them his new invention."

"What is it?"

"He's made a robotic talking head out of one of my aunt's styrofoam heads. It's great! It has eyes that move and a synthetic voice. He says it could help as a teaching tool one day. The kids will love it. He'll let them record their voices for it."

"I would be a terrible mother if I cheated them out of *that*," she says. "I just hope they don't get nightmares."

"No. Couldn't scare a soul. Too ridiculous looking."

"Okay. But I owe you. *Big time.*"

"Speaking of big time," I segue, "the concert's coming up. How are you feeling about staying up a little later than usual?"

"Like I can't."

"Oh, Helen!"

"Brad has arranged for a limo to pick us up and bring us home, but ..."

"We can leave early. We can leave just as soon as you want."

I stop because her expression says, *Please, I can't.*

"It's not going to be the same," says Joan, "without her."

"I know. What about if we had the concert at her house?"

"Good idea. I'll call their manager and suggest it."

"No," Joan laughs. "Maybe they have some live CDs, and we can skip the concert and just go to her house and play them loud."

"Oh! Maybe we can take a ride in the limo first, then go back to her house. That would be fun!"

"We can still get all dressed up, as if we were going. Helen too."

"An *un*concert!" I say happily.

"What should we do about the tickets?"

"Well, we could ... let's see ... oh, I know! Let's give them to the clinic where she has her treatments. There must be three Earth, Wind & Fire fans there who would love to go!"

"Perfect. Brad said he and Helen wanted to do something for them."

We're disappointed when Helen isn't even up for the ride. "But come back afterward," she says. "I'm not in a dancing mood but will love to have you around the house with me."

"Only if you want us," I say. "But it's a bit much. A stretch limo for two? Just Joan and me?"

"I do want you here," she says. "And when you take it to the streets, as they say, who says it's going to be just the two of you Chicks? I have a surprise for you."

"A surprise? What *kind* of surprise? A good surprise or a ..."

"You'll see."

The spring air is filled with the scent of jasmine in bloom as the limo pulls up to my front yard. Joan's tight, black cocktail dress is loaded with sequins and has a slit up to her thigh. For someone whose kitchen produces the highest caloric item found in any bakery, she never wears any of them on her hips.

"Where are your stilettos?" she asks me.

"Can't wear them," I say. "Fear of heights."

"I should have guessed."

We get in, like stepping from day into the dark of night, welcomed by spacious, sensual leather and mirrors sprinkled with gold highlights, a full bar, and ...

"Good evening, ladies!" says a great-looking man decked out in a tux.

"Jim?" I gasp. "Where did *you* come from?"

He's not alone. Brad is there too, and someone else, and their martini glasses are already half empty. Big grins suggest that they're having a good time and feeling no pain. The song on the CD player is "Shining Star."

"Have a seat, you—Chicks," says Brad. "We're all going for a spin around the highways before you go back to Helen."

"But first," says Jim, "you need a drink." He opens the bar, and it's stocked with everything.

"Sorry! This is Mike," says Brad, nodding at the third man. "Just moved to town and opened a new business."

"Brad set him up with a loan," Jim tries to explain. But Mike doesn't seem to mind, just smiles and nods.

"What kind of business?" asks Joan.

"I think you'd like it. Sweet Cakes."

Joan does not respond well to this term of endearment and sends me a look that asks, *Is this supposed to be my date for the night?*

"You ought to come by," Mike says.

"What's the name?" Joan asks politely.

"Um ... Sweet Cakes. Is the name."

Joan's eyes grow wide. "*Ohhh* ... the new bakery! You're the ..."

"Owner. It's nice to meet you. I've tasted your buns." The guys take a quick look at Mike and laugh. "No, I mean, they're really delicious."

More guffaws. "Stop, Mike. You're killing us!" says Brad.

"Oh, *you* stop it, you juvenile delinquents," Joan says. "Thank you, Mike."

"It's not a night for business. But come by sometime, and let's talk."

The next thing you know, she's sitting next to him, deep in conversation.

"You guys are great," I say to Jim and Brad.

"It was Helen's idea."

Joan hears that and looks over. "To Helen," she says, raising her glass of whatever it was Jim handed her. We toast to Helen, then to each other. Then to the driver, who keeps the Earth, Wind & Fire hits coming.

For the next couple of hours, we are driven all around the Bay Area, not paying attention to where we are but with an eye on the time. We want to give Helen plenty of time to rest but not get there so late that she's tired again.

She's subdued but happy to see us. And we are all together. As we dance and sing and laugh, nothing is certain but this alive and glorious moment in time—together, as the Chicks in Charge.

Winds of Change

I OPEN MY EYES and face the same thoughts I took to bed. Nighttime played a mixed score of old memories with twisted outcomes and voices of long ago, making efforts to sleep futile.

"Rough night?" Jim asks, nicely acknowledging the obvious as he silences the alarm clock. He'd woken a time or two, muttering, "Whoa! *Stop!*" while trying to defend himself from my thrashings.

"Time to get up? I finally fell asleep about five minutes ago."

"I think I'm bruised," he says, rubbing his arm. "So, was it a bad dream? Tell me what it was." He always comes to my aid after a nightmare to let me know how it's really not something to worry about. But he won't be able to today. And I can't tell him my dreams because I know what they mean, what they're related to. I must practice stalls today—the maneuver I've been avoiding—on my own.

"Nothing. Just a lot of ... random thoughts," I lie.

When he gets up, I stay in bed, staring at the ceiling, trying to recall dreams that felt so real, which were so real once upon a time.

In my dream, I feel the wind blowing on my face, hear the sound of metal on concrete. Rolling faster and faster on shoe-attached roller skates as a five-year-old, I am connected by a long rope to the collar of my mother's dog, who, inspired by a rare chance of outdoor freedom, happily pulls me at his full dachshund speed. He turns a corner and, instead of heading into the street, I let go and careen up a steep driveway, grateful to be slowing down. But last night the ending changed. Suddenly, coming toward me are a few cars, then several more, then roads of cars, horns blaring, their bumpers only inches from my small form.

I awake, relieved to realize it is only a vision, but minutes later my head falls back into the whirlpool.

I am nine. In our working-class neighborhood, the kids have a scrappiness that usually serves us well. After all, a certain amount of moxie is a quality necessary if you want to get picked for the street's kickball teams headed by the boys, one of their many inventive games that hold infinitely more interest for me than dolls or baking. At dusk, in the summertime, and still filled with energy to spare, our scrap sometimes leads to dare. That night, Johnny Burton, two years younger, says that my terrier is ugly, and no one can call the dog I loved ugly, even if he most definitely is.

"Take it *back!*" I demand.

"*Make* me!" he shouts. He puts up his fists, and I freeze.

At the same time, his mom calls him home for dinner. When he yells back, "Be right there!" I knock him across the sidewalk with an instinctive foot punch, honed by several summer weeks of playing kickball. His friends' laughter adds to his humiliation.

Then the dream warps into a different ending with his gang of friends running after me, and me trying to outrun a mob, hoping I can still climb up and over fences and remember the old neighborhood well enough to find the right hiding places. I am panting, hearing them come closer.

Finally, turning from that nightmare, I hear the words from the doctor. Not one doctor but others—all in a chorus, repeating the same thing: "It's your call," they tell me, looking at my aunt. "It's your call."

I wake to their echo.

Stall practice. Alone inside, I will make Bravo lose the wind over her wings and arrest our forward motion. I can already hear the warning horn scream into the air as we begin our fall to Earth. The rudders and I will kick the airplane into balance. In those moments I will be in command to either continue my life or meet its end.

"I know this," I say to this new kind of stage fright. "Put your mental tray into its full, upright, and locked position. The captain has turned on your emotional seat belt sign. Fasten it. And remember to breathe."

Before leaving the house to take my children to school and go to the airfield, I sneak a call to Marge from the Ninety-Nines.

Ring … ring … ring … Please be there, Marge. Pick up.

"Hello?"

"Thank goodness. It's MJ, Marge. I need to tell you something."

"Are you okay?"

"I have to go up and stall the airplane. By myself. I wanted to tell you. Because you know what I'm talking about."

"I do."

"I'm scared of doing them. Maybe that tells me something. That I'm not ready."

"You're supposed to be scared. I was too. Everyone is at first. Takes doing a lot of them, to tell the truth. They're my least favorite maneuver. Most of us feel that way."

"What if it spins? What if it stalls, then goes into a spin? It happened to one of my classmates a couple of months ago—John. He told me he finally pulled out but barely in time. Said he had put too much rudder into the maneuver, and the airplane stalled, then delivered a nose-down spiral for him. Said all he saw was the ground below." I pause to wonder where he's been. "He said he needed some time off after that but hasn't been back in a while."

"Listen! You are *not* John. You've shown them to instructors. You've practiced them in your head. You won't spin. You'll control it. Then you'll fix it," Marge says. "Knowing them is like knowing CPR for airplanes. Like blowing life back into their bodies."

I linger after chatting with Blake and Annie in front of the school. The halls echo with school-day memories of my own. The school bell explodes today the way it did long ago, in its bugle-call way to start another day. All the small figures scurry to line up, with teachers meeting them at the thresholds of their classrooms. There were times I entered with dread to meet the challenges of the day. Would it be a test day of difficulty and end in doom or bring proud achievement? Every schoolkid has a moment when they feel like running away—like I feel now.

155

I turn to go back to my car and then to the airfield when I unexpectedly hear, "Just who I wanted to see!" Another mom waves to me, clad in a beautiful, new aviator jacket of soft, light-tan leather. "What do you think, huh?" she asks with her arms out to show me.

"Nice." I hardly know her. Her daughter runs with the popular crowd of kids. This mom runs around with the popular crowd's moms. "Did you just get it?"

"Yes. In preparation for *flying* lessons!" she says gleefully.

"Really? That's ... well, great! I didn't know you were interested."

"Well, we all know *you're* a flying student now, and I thought, 'How cool is *that*? I should look into that too!' I'd *love* to talk sometime. But how do I look? And, you know, since my divorce," she continues in a softer voice, "I'd like a place where I can meet new people."

"I'm on my way now. To the airfield, that is."

She looks carefully at my tan cotton jacket, now with oil stains that won't fully wash out. Then her furrowed brow vanishes into a wide smile again. "Well, I bet you go there all the time. What are you learning these days? Is it great to be in the sky? Like a bird? Is it a lot of work?"

I look at her. "A lot of—work?" She needs more hope than a real reply. "It's—challenging. Like today ..." *No. Don't tell her.* "... will be another wonderful day up there!" I say. "Need to go. Let me know when you'd like to talk more."

"I'd *love* that!"

As I walk to my car, I hear, "Hey! What do you think? It's a *real* flight jacket ..."

"Another wonderful day," I repeat as I roll into a steep turn to look around my practice area.

MJ: "Approach, 83Bravo at 5,000. Maneuvering."

I give myself an extra couple of thousand feet, in case I need it to get out—of trouble. I'm on my third peppermint.

Radar Control: "83Bravo, squawk 5252."

I enter the numbers in the transponder to stay on their radar screens. They know maneuvering means that I'll be doing lots of circling, cuts into the air, and altitude changes in the area. They'll help keep watch over the skies.

The wind is from the west. If I fly into it, the recovery is a little easier, giving more wind over the wings.

"I will begin my setup to stall the plane." But don't. I fly out of my practice area, stalling about stalling. I circle back into the practice zone. "Set it up." *Go. Set it up. Watch the needles. Stay on the rudders.*

My knees start to shudder. I set up the stall into the west wind again. The headlands are in the distance. "Keep the nose on the headlands." Because the recovery must be in the heading where it started—not way off to one side like a cloud, helpless and drifting.

"Begin." I say. "I will … start. Now!" I keep going and am out of the practice area again. *Turn around. Go back. Go back.* I turn around to start again.

Get the west heading. Now 500 feet higher. Go down, pull the power. Find the 5,000 again. Stay west. "Begin a power-off stall." I leave the power alone. I put my hand on the throttle and leave it there, feeling its round size, the steel rod beyond the knob, and twist it a little right, then left. Then squeeze it. I look at my watch. *I know how to do this.*

"A full power-out stall. Begin!" I hesitate. "Now!" Carb heat goes on, mixture in, power out, flaps, nose up, more flaps. I see the needle slowly dropping as the airspeed bleeds off, and the nose goes skyward further and further.

Bravo's horn screeches, then screams—it is a dying airplane. There is hardly any control I have except for the rudders. My feet put some pressure on the left, then the right, then the left. The stick has lost its use. *Feel it.* The air breaks away from the wings, and Bravo's nose falls downward and to the left from lack of lift, from a mechanical design to favor leftward.

"Recovering …" Then quickly, "Carb off and full power, flaps one, nose up and level, wings level, flaps two …" I feel strength in the airplane. We are, once again, flying. The full tenor of Bravo's voice has returned.

"Yes!" I am still heading west. And still inside the practice zone. "Lost 300 feet on that try. Not too bad." *I need to try to keep it to 100. I can do better.* "Let's do it again." I look at my watch: all that inside one minute.

When I return to school to pick up Blake and Annie, I see the same mom there, still wearing her stylish flight attire.

"How …" she says, looking me over, somewhat dismayed, "… did it go today?" It might be my disheveled hair and slash of sunburn across my face from looking skyward today for so long.

"Another wonderful day up there," I answer.

Long, cross-country trips take a lot of time to prepare. *Where will I go?*

"Take yourself into the foothills of the Sierra," says Captain Lee. "It separates the men …" he begins, then stops.

"From the better pilots?" I suggest, remaining cordial.

"The foothills have illusions," he shrugs. "On the west side of the Placerville runway is a canyon. It plays tricks, dropping down hundreds of feet below." To dramatize, he makes a slicing, downward motion with his hand. "Gives pilots the illusion that they are too high and should fly lower."

"Okay. Thanks for telling me not to fall for it," I say. *I'll show him. I'll put that one on my list of possibilities.*

Preparations include watching the long-range weather forecasts. So far the week ahead is clear, with thunderstorms in the mountains; more avoidable if I fly in the morning. I'll plan to stop where I can get fuel, get out to stretch, and get to see who's around.

In the evenings I review my emergency cards: *What will I do if I see the oil pressure drop or the temperature rise; if the engine calls it quits; if I have another audio time-out or have my private comments broadcast far and wide?* I look at where I can go; not a lot of glide room in the tree-topped mountains, the ones with deep canyons that I don't want to end up inside. I make time to visit the mechanic to be sure all is updated and rechecked.

"I don't want to be resting on a treetop," I tell the mechanics in the hangar. "I don't want to give Captain Lee the pleasure."

This flight of over 200 miles will start right after sunrise—a journey that will test a thousand things I have learned. It will take several hours, including stops I need to make. I will leave from my home airfield and land at two others: one in the foothills of Gold Country; the other deep into the agricultural heart of the Central Valley. Days and days of preparation have

158

included all the details, large and small: headings, adjustments based on the forecasted wind changes, and diagrams and mental practicing for the arrivals. I have made several cards that will be placed on a secure clipboard.

Bravo has full tanks, a clean windscreen, and a less faded red stripe since I saw to it that it got a coat of wax. Opening the airplane's door to the fragrances of flight inside, I place on the empty seat next to me two navigation charts, full plans on well-battened-down note cards, water bottles, a few energy bars, and Helen's small dragon, which I have named "Flaps."

The sky is a clean, clear blue. Turf between runways is neatly trimmed; I saw the mower working below when I came in to land the other day. The mix of sweet grasses and purple lupine from nearby fields rises to fill the air, like the scent of freshly washed linen. Earlier spring rains have nudged the hillsides, offering up yellow mustard flowers. The day is splendid though not forecast to be perfect. On my flight back to Concord, strong breezes with high, racing clouds will try their best to push me back.

"Clear!" I shout out Bravo's window and bring the propeller to life. We taxi out, checking the engine gauges one more time. Within minutes, we leave the ground, rising, to head to the first destination: the hidden airfield in the foothills, nestled on a precipice with a canyon below.

"Trust your altimeter," Kevin had told me. "Keep it set to current air pressure. Ask for updates from the controller."

Flying toward the Sierra range. The hills that years ago lured prospectors to seek their fortunes of gold now pass the hours in peace, welcoming hikers, backpackers, and daring rock climbers who hang by ropes. *What kind of person would want to do that?* Tucked in the folds leading up to the higher hills, old oaks gather; over the hours, their shadows swing around them like dark capes. Hills, once wearing fall colors of brown suede, have new spring wardrobes of green velvet. Seeing this from above casts an everlasting spell.

My airplane and I rise with the rising landscape. Oaks give way to conifers. I look down on endless horizons of towering pines, like wide lawns of sturdy blades of grass. I keep an eye out for a rock quarry, my landmark that I am on target for my first stop. I don't see it.

I call to a nontowered airfield, which is usually monitored by a devotee: "Placerville, 5483Bravo 20 miles southwest. Landing, looking for traffic advisories. Placerville."

A delay. I check the frequency dialed and hear a distinct voice.

Monitor: "83Bravo. Advise north runway. And, tell me, what's your aircraft?"

MJ: "83Bravo is a Cessna 152."

Monitor: "Right. You're a little thing. Okay! I'll look for you."

"Don't listen to him, Bravo," I say to the airplane.

Finally, beyond the trees, against a cliff, is the quarry. Near it, a drop-off to a low and deep canyon. I watch the altimeter. The airfield appears, almost carved into the hillside. I make a downwind turn to the south and continue to watch the runway off my left side. I trust the altimeter, trying to ignore the rocky depth below me. On my final turn, Placerville airfield looms larger, and Bravo and I make a squeak of a touchdown. Taxiing to the fuel pump, I pop open my window, and the mountain morning cools off my downwind worries.

In less than an hour, I've arrived in a new land of wonder. This airfield is small. The air is pure. And, since it's Thursday, it is quiet, with many small planes tied down, asleep, waiting for their weekend pilots to return. To one side, forest fire-fighting aircraft stand ready for what may come in the dry summer months.

"Howdy, there!" comes a voice, the one I heard over my headset. Bounding across the ramp comes its owner. "I'm Hank! Welcome to heaven!" His grin sports a missing tooth, and his sun-worn skin creases at the corners of his eyes. A threadbare flannel shirt matches his years of time. He holds out his hand. It has the feel of strong leather.

"I'm MJ. Nice to meet you, Hank."

"So this here's your Bravo, huh? Nice," he says, looking it over from nose to tail. "Never met an airplane I didn't like. And let me guess. You're on your long cross-country."

"Yes, I am. Do I look it?"

"I know your airplane. Never forget one neither. Bravo's been up here before." I look over at Bravo, impressed with her history and sustained courage to make these journeys with endless numbers of student pilots. "Was a time when I'd have to sign your logbook to verify you made it. One of them many old rules that's gone away. But at least the airstrip's still here."

Like most who have seen the way it was and now the way it is, I hear his preference. Looking westward with him, across his runways, the foothills, and further out to the distant broad valleys, I agree. We are standing on an airfield that gazes on infinity.

"Have you been here a long time, Hank? In Placerville?" I ask, wishing I had all morning to hear his stories. I set up Bravo to receive more fuel.

"Years back, I thought I'd stay a spell, get my fill of airplanes and the mountains that surround us. Then I'd move on to make my fortune. Or at least, a better fortune. Not much money in this line of work." He looks at me with a fleeting sadness, then brightens. "How many hours you got now?"

"About 80."

"Bet you learned something from each of them hours." When I nod, he goes on. "Mine's measured in decades. More like epochs. From wartime to peacetime. From slow aircraft to fast."

"And your favorite? Of all the airplanes?"

"Right over there. My Waco. Best bi-wing ever made. Rolling and looping for years now." It's a stunning red masterpiece, with the leading edges of the wings trimmed in blue. "When I fly her, I hear full orchestras playin'." *I know! I hear that too.* "But—time's up."

"Time's up?" I look to see if the refueling pump is finished. Running low on fuel when I am her pilot will not happen to Bravo ever again.

"I mean it's time to sell it."

"*Sell* it? What? The field? Your Waco?"

"The Waco and the airfield business. Everything. Could make lots of money on the sale of them. Makes lots of sense too. Who needs the problems? The expenses?" A telephone bell rings from an old, black phone on the wall inside his office. "Got to get that. Come in for a minute."

I jog after him into a small lobby leading to a wider room that's a page taken from aviation's past. Old, wooden propellers hang in every corner, and hand-painted on them are the names and years of the airplanes they were once attached to. On the walls, black-and-white pictures of pilots, with their arms around the shoulders of their buddies, all smiles, airplanes in the background.

"You bet I'll be here," Hank says to the caller. "I'll look at that gauge for you. Bet I know what's wrong with it." He hangs up and makes a few notes with a pencil.

"This is like walking inside a book, Hank. Who are all these pilots?"

"These pilots are all my friends. And their airplanes too. Tell you what? I'll snap a Polaroid of you and Bravo before you go and add it to my wall!" We walk out to Bravo, and Hank pushes the button. In minutes, a wet, black-and-white, ghostly view of Bravo and me darkens into a real picture. "There! You will join Hank's Hall of Fame of pilots and the airplanes they love."

"I'll see you again when I come back," I tell Hank, feeling certain about it.

"Good deal. Fly safe! And keep it up!" he says with a laugh—a joke he probably tells several times a week. The phone in his office rings again. "Got to get that." He runs to the lobby. "Hey there. When you flying in?"

Through the window I see him smiling.

I crawl back into my airplane and taxi over to where I landed to begin my takeoff roll. The airfield of heaven falls away as do the canyons below, which will have to wait for another pair of pilot eyes to try and fool. My journey continues, far southward across the vast agricultural span of California.

The pine trees change to fruit and nut orchards and fields of produce. Being a few thousand feet in the air, unlike the heights commercial airlines must make, allows me to see the individual trees—acres and acres of them—all looking like Brussels sprouts that someone laid out in perfect patterns.

A couple of times along the way, I call the radar service for vectors to be sure my headings are on course. But it's more—I like to hear their voice;

to know they're there; that they know I filed a solo flight and that I'm up here.

The winds must be picking up. I calculate my true airspeed, which is slower than what the airspeed indicator shows. With the needle showing Bravo hitting the lightspeed of 100 miles an hour, it will still take at least an hour to get to Merced. *Enjoy the view. But think of where to land. Just in case.*

Coming in for my second landing, I find that another pilot is also landing there. Since there is no tower or field assistant like Hank to help us, we talk to each other through our headsets to decide who will land first and where we will taxi off. I mention that I'm a student pilot on a cross-country trip.

"Great! You stopping for a break?" the other pilot asks.

"I can." I am going to make it a fast one this time.

"Look for me inside. I'm meeting a friend of mine."

"See you."

I land and tie down Bravo next to the other pilot's airplane—a handsome and nostalgic Cub of yellow fabric; a tail wheel, tandem design. As I run my finger on the soft canvas, I think, *I'd love to have you.*

I walk up to the small café just as two cowboys exit and tip their hats to me. I smile but don't dare turn around because I think they're still looking.

I hear, "Think she's a pilot?"

And his friend answers, "Betcha. *Looove* them lady pilots."

Their spirited voices and stomping boots fade as they go out to the airplanes. I've entered aviation's mildly Wild West.

"Hi!" says the pilot, who was in the other plane coming in. He and his friend are sitting in a booth. They rise a little out of their seats to acknowledge me. One slides over to let me in. "I'm George. This here's Jack."

The sign outside says "Café," but the place feels more like a saloon. Country Western music is playing on the radio. Mementoes on the walls are a montage of horses, steer, and serious-looking cowboys with their arms crossed as they stand in front of aircraft on the ramp outside.

"I'm MJ."

"Oh, no," moans George. "Not *MJ*. Lost my heart to a girl who went by 'MJ.' Never gotten over it."

"That was forever ago. Time to get over it, George," says Jack.

The waitress comes over and delivers their coffee in white, coffee-stained, porcelain mugs. Then puts her hands on her hips, looks at them both, rolls her eyes, and shakes her head. I doubt she's really as annoyed as she puts on.

"Sally, this here's MJ. One day I'm going to get over the girl who broke my heart with that name."

Sally looks at me and winks. "What would you like, honey? We've got the grill going." I ask her for a ginger ale. "You got it," she says to me. "Boys, you ordering the usual?"

"Yep. The usual, Sally." She walks away. "So, tell us. How did you get the flying bug? Your boyfriend do it? Your husband?" asks Jack with a piercing but friendly look.

"No. I do it because I need to. It's filling a dream and ..."

"Now *that's* my kind of gal!" says George. "One who fills a dream."

"Every gal is your kind of gal. But they's *smart* enough to know you is *not* their kind of guy," says Jack, perturbed. Then back to me says, "What will you do with it? With flying, that is. We two have done lots of jobs with flying."

The waitress brings my soda. "They're harmless. Just crazy," she tells me softly.

"I'm enjoying it mostly," I answer back to the men. "It's challenging and ..."

"Well, now, I love it too. When I get some extra cash, I'm going to get a modern airplane. One with all the latest GPSs. Then I can get an even better job," says George.

"A *better* one? You ain't got one now!" says Jack. "You done gambled away your fancy new plane." Then looks my way again, like George disappears and can't hear him. "Keeps going up to Reno. Putting it down. And seeing it go."

"Next time. Next time," George insists. "My luck's going to change. My wife will be so pleased with me. And you'll be *begging* me for a ride in my new *Cirrus*," he says to Jack as he sits up straighter.

"Go on," says Jack and then to me. "She hates airplanes. She's going to clip his wings if he keeps a gamblin' away the funds."

"I'd love to fly that Cub you have. Jack, what do you do?" I ask, turning his way.

"Skywritin'," he says proudly. "Used to be a crop duster. But changed to writin'. Write out all sorts of things. Marriage proposals, apologies …"

"Yeah. Follows the marriage proposing," quips George.

"And even quoted words from God his self," says Jack, glaring at George.

I cough a little on my soda. "Sorry. The fizz. From God himself?"

"Well, from the customer who says God says," explains Jack. "These days, I've gone high tech," nodding to both of us with smug assurance. "I relay them down to people from below my wings. I rigged it so it's all digitized and very high tech. So I been doing a lot of night flying. To get the messages seen."

"What kind of messages?" I ask.

"Lately I get jobs that advertise. The kids love to point up and see me fly overhead with my blinking messages. They're about insurance: 'Don't Go Uncovered.'"

"Insurance." Puzzled, I ask, "Do kids know what that is?"

Jack fidgets a bit and tucks in his shirt. "*Hmm*. Maybe not. No matter though. It gets their attention. Besides, in today's world, not many can do what I do. I'm unique."

George takes delight in his friend's talent and confidence. "We should pool our resources, Jack. Do something steady. Using your good, high-tech skills and the new airplane I'll have soon." Then he looks at me. "And if you'd like to join our business, when you're licensed and all, give a holler. We'll be here. We're here most every day."

Sally brings their grilled sandwiches and chips and refills their coffees.

"When I'm good enough. One day," I say, getting up from the booth. The men rise a little out of their seats. I reach in my pocket to pay for the soda.

"Nope! Stop right there. I got that," says George.

"*We* got that," corrects Jack, with a hard look at George. He puts his finger on my soda tab and pulls it toward his lunch plate.

"Thank you. Thank you both," I say. "You're gentlemen. And pilots."

"Did you hear that?" George says as I go. "'Gentlemen,' the lady said. MJ of my past, where did you go?" he croons, with a hint of real melancholy.

"Get *over* it," says his friend.

I head out, through the swinging café door, to see Bravo waiting. As I exit, a couple more cowboys enter from the ramp, tipping their hats. I could get use to that.

Before I leave, I check Bravo all over, outside and inside, like it's the start of the day. Listening to the engine, the magnetos sound rough. A common problem, but I still need to burn off the carbon. I reach for the checklist I made on how to clear them. *Fixed.*

The windsock on the Merced airfield is catching a brisk breeze. I ramble down to the takeoff end with the breeze on Bravo's nose, pop a peppermint, and begin the final leg of my journey.

Coursing along the west side of the interior valley I watch for other aircraft first, then compare the navigation chart to the land below. Clusters of towns, small and large, dot the landscape all the way out to the horizon. Buildings and houses look like pieces from a board game. I match the small airports to the map.

Modesto! I should say hello as I fly over. Instead, I check my list to be sure I've done all that needs to be done. *No!* I forgot to check in with radar control. *They are not going to be happy ...*

MJ: "Radar Control, 5483Bravo with you abeam ..."

Radar Control: "5483Bravo! Where have you been? You're off your schedule. You *must* sign off with us. Or we'll send out someone to look for you!"

166

MJ: "Yes. Sir. Sorry. Won't happen again. 83Bravo." I snap off quickly.

When I'm closer to Concord and the frequency signals are within reach, I will listen to the wind and airfield information. The day is later than planned, the sun hotter, and I want to open the air vents. I put the clipped-down cards and all the other paperwork on the empty seat next to me and top them off with an airport guidebook. Then I put Flaps the dragon on top of the whole stack. His felt tongue flutters in the airflow of the vents like he's laughing.

The closer I get, the slower Bravo goes. Looking down on a ribbon of highway, the speed of the slower cars is my actual speed, with the wind pushing back on the airplane. My landmark mountain—Diablo, a symbol of home—is taking forever to near. The airfield updates tell me I will need to cross the glittering reservoir that leads to the runway. Today, its wind-blown ripples tell me that a crosswind landing is in store and will need some extra power, and to use less flaps. All the way down, gusts buffet and bounce us.

Bravo noses to the right side of the runway. *Keep on the centerline. Don't hurry.* I make a final rudder adjustment and put the aileron into the wind. The number 19 looms larger.

"Bravo! We did it!"

Tower: "83Bravo, proceed directly to the ramp," says the ground controller. "MJ?"

MJ: "Martin? Just finished my long cross-country!"

Tower: "You rock! I mean, proceed to the ramp."

I bring Bravo into a parking place, take down the numbers for the time of the flight—3.25—and jump out. Closing the door, I see … *Is that Will?* I notice his uniform. Four stripes are on his epaulets.

I greet him and say, "They've made you a captain!" But he doesn't show similar enthusiasm. "It's so *great* to see you!"

"You too. Your training coming along, okay? Testing soon?"

"Soon. I just took a personal tour of California. Or should I say learned from its many personalities."

"What's *that* mean?"

I tell him about the man in charge of the heaven he thinks he will sell, the gambler who has a dream, and his friend the skywriter.

"I just came back from more than a long flight." But I see that his mind's on other things. "How are your students at the academy, Will?"

"Fine," he says distractedly. "But not like you guys." He leans against Bravo and looks down.

"You heard about Tom?"

"Yeah. Terrible. A real shame."

"He loved it, Will. You helped with that, you know. You helped me too. In the early months, going up with you." I want to bottle the exhilaration of the takeoffs and give it to him. He deserves to know the difference he's made, my first guide to the skies. The heavens unfolded before me and haven't stopped since. "We're proud of you, Will. Your move up."

"Is that what it was?"

"Isn't it?"

"I guess. So what are your plans? Planning to continue? After your test?"

"Of course." I gather all my papers, secure Bravo with a pat on her propeller, and Will and I stroll back to the flight school.

"You should go for your instrument rating. Beyond that too." Instrument flight: the ultimate video game, learning to fly in clouds and fog.

"Me? Are you *kidding*? No. I'm not the Top Gun material you're teaching now. I'm just ... just a pilot—*almost* a pilot—in love with it."

He opens the door to let me in with my heavier-than-usual flight bag. "I'm here to see if I can come back as an instructor."

"What?" I pull him back outside so we can't be heard. "You are? Are you *sure*? Because, if you're sure, I might continue." He smiles widely. "I'm warning you. I might!"

"And I'd rather teach someone in love with it than work as a logbook endorser. I'm teaching at a pilot factory. I'd rather teach people who see that there's more to it than ..." He looks down at my flight bag. "Is that—a dragon?" he asks, seeing Flaps on top of my notes.

"Yes. Yes, it is," I stammer. "Of course. Everyone should take one along on their flights."

"What have you been learning since I've been gone?"

I look at him. "Let's see. Where should I start? Have you heard of pilot eyes?"

"Tell me about it over a cup of coffee, long-distance flyer."

Pilot Eyes

MY TASK THIS MORNING is simple: a straightforward flight to a small Sacramento airport, go over the hills, buzz across the wide-open valley, tell the tower I'm landing, and … there. *Done.* Then return. *Simple.* I should make this flight spectacular since I am closing in on final exams for pilothood. Which means Kevin is closing in on parenthood. Between us is the air of nervous anticipation for what the future holds.

Running behind time, I gather my flight bag from my car and grab some charts, notebooks, and my 10-ton textbook—I don't know why; it just always goes along. I give Flaps a squeeze and throw him in the bag. Then, on second thought, take him out again.

"Wait here," I say, and close the trunk.

Inside I get the aviation reports for the current weather for both departing and arriving airfields: A cold front is forecast for later in the day. Small aircraft advisories will be issued if needed. I look at the probability: Chances are slim. Look at the system in color on a radar screen: A triangle-edged arch shifts slightly, with mounting potential during the warm part of the afternoon, many hours away. *Fine. We'll be back long before then.*

Now airborne, we're on our way. Kevin begins to rub his knees. "Say aloud the arrival checklist," he instructs automatically. *I wonder if he has one for his baby too.*

I race through the information of five As—ATIS, altimeter, airspeed, altitude, arrival runway—at a speed an auctioneer would envy.

Kevin gives a slight nod of approval. His knees are now well polished.

"How's your wife feeling?" I ask as I crane my neck to look for the airfield. Seeing it, I begin my descent. Ahead and from the northwest, a distant mass of clouds is barely visible.

"Good, good. Any day now," I hear him say as he looks outside too. "Hmm, interesting clouds way out there."

The Sacramento runways loom larger. My heart gives a leap to see it as planned. I love the welcome sight of an airfield. They are dear to my heart, and each is a field for dreams, where wheels roll and wings fly.

"Let's land, then taxi off to the ramp," he says, "for a short talk about your exams and what your examiner wants to see you do."

I nod. We're cleared to taxi over to the other rows of airplanes. They're tied down but some not firmly enough. Wings gently rock.

"You need to know how to make safe navigation deviations. Be ready for a change he'll make to your plans. To see if you get rattled. To see how you think. So say it out loud."

"I had that fog event, remember? Got that nailed."

"Be sure you can calculate fuel reserves fast. And know how to figure your distance, power setting, and speed for descents. And don't bluff! Even though you've studied a lot. There's always more."

"Will it count against me if I say I don't know?"

"No one knows it all, even though some act like they do. He'll press to see how far he can take you with his questions. When you're out of your depth, stop. An honest pilot knows their limits."

"Okay."

"Should we go inside the airport office before we head back? Check their screens for any new reports?"

"All covered," I say, patting the pages I printed earlier. I'm sitting in the left seat—the seat of the pilot in command. "Let's go back."

Minutes later, I align Bravo for takeoff. We are on our way to complete the morning lesson. *Straightforward. Simple.*

Radar Control: "Notice to all airmen," says a serious voice, in real time, over our radio. Kevin and I exchange glances. "Airmet Tango in the vicinity southwest of Sacramento." Our area has received a weather warning for strong turbulence for all small aircraft—like Bravo. The storm shouldered in and is forcing itself our way. "Notice to all airmen ..." the warning repeats. Reading about these warnings is nothing compared to how I feel about getting one.

Bravo quickly reacts to this news with a few hard bounces from the local convective current that's inhaling the air above. A mass of growing clouds with black edges is distinct and expanding, telltales that they are feeding on the moist atmosphere; unbridled and wild, they are lifted to greater heights on rising backs of heat. Thunder rumbles.

"Shhhhit!" Kevin articulates calmly as he stares outside.

"God!" I gasp, stunned to see something like this at eye level moving with such menace. It is outside our window, less than a few a miles away, with an extended claw of black attached to a larger body, contorted but growing. It is a monster. A thunderhead. *A thunderhead? At this time of day? In this area?*

We take action. "You fly," I tell Kevin. He draws back some power from Bravo and tries to hold our altitude as Bravo tries to endure fists of turbulence. "I've got the radios."

"Call in. Get some vectors."

I've forgotten the proper wording. *Screw it!*

MJ: "Approach, this is 5483Bravo. A C152. Storm in our area. Advise with vectors?" I hear my voice, but it sounds like someone else trying to control a desperate plea.

Approach: "83Bravo. Have you on radar, southwest of Sacramento," comes a serene reply. Then stops.

MJ: "Approach ..." I begin again. *Maybe he forgot me, or I missed something. He's taking forever!* "App—"

Approach: "83Bravo. Storm in your vicinity of flight. Severe. Suggest turning left, 1-7-0."

Kevin begins the turn.

MJ: "83Bravo, turning 1-7-0," I repeat.

Approach: "83Bravo, say number of souls aboard."

A fierce set of bumps jolts Bravo off course. I don't think Bravo is built for this.

"83Bravo. Two—on board." I close my eyes for a moment. They have to ask in case they have to come looking. "Approach, our preference, to get into Concord. What's your radar show?" In the gloom, I flip on our landing light, a dim candlelight behind a dark curtain. *Options.* We must run from it, not outrun it to the same base.

Approach: "83Bravo, I'm showing red north of the field."

MJ: "83Bravo."

Then to Kevin, "What do you think?"

"We'll stay south of it, just in time."

Still growing to a whipping, rising power, it begins to release reservoirs of rain. Wide, grey sheets fall in the distance. Bravo's propeller chases away the few first drops cast out to us, but it won't be able to clear steady rainfall, and we won't be able to see through it. It will be slow going too.

"Stay south. I'll call Concord." *We will do this right. This will not be the day my children get a phone call from the airfield.* I switch frequencies and begin without the customary language.

MJ: "Concord Tower, 5483Bravo. Ten miles east. Strong turbulence in the area. Difficult to keep level. Landing. Need 19Left."

Tower: "83Bravo. Are you declaring an emergency?"

MJ: "We are next to the storm …"

I look out to our right to see it. A dark eye looks back so close I can almost reach out to touch it. I hesitate. *Is life at risk?* I look at Kevin. He shakes his head. I look outside again. We are shoulder to shoulder with a side of nature I have never seen look so crazed or so malevolent. An invisible knee of wind knocks into Bravo. Tossed upward I hear the airplane send out its stall horn, but just as fast Bravo's nose falls back down with a snap. Kevin's head slams against the ceiling.

"Ouch! You bastard!" he calls to the monster outside.

"Kevin?"

"I'm fine. Fine." He rubs his head. "I've got the plane."

Tower: "83Bravo. Are you declaring an emergency?"

MJ: "83Bravo requests …" I give it another moment. "… Priority landing. Turbulence is severe."

"No!" says Kevin.

But I've overridden his call. I have the left seat. The storm is too strong, too uncertain, and too close. And too personal: I need to preserve two parents and a bold, little airplane that's as tired of this merciless slapping as we are. *What if the storm throws a knockout punch?* I have asked for priority—that's urgent. An emergency. The whole airfield will react to this. The emergency assistance trucks will arrive; any other aircraft will have to circle. All waiting. Watching for Bravo to make it in.

"Landing checklist," he says.

Over the airways, we hear Concord announce to all aircraft in the vicinity that severe turbulence is reported. Bravo has been cleared to land.

I read over the checklist and notice that it's quaking in my hand. Unsure, I repeat the list and prepare for our descent from a sky possessed by a dragon.

Bravo's wheels arrive over the centerline as a sudden, final gust pushes us to the left. We are still on the runway but barely. The grass median is under the left wing. Just then the whole runway is swept by rain, making taxiing almost impossible.

"It just goes to show," Kevin begins, as we pull Bravo up to her parking spot and stop. I know he's going to chew me out for my incomplete weather report, for my decision to declare an emergency. "No two flying days are alike. Or even two flying hours," he says. "Nice job."

"What?"

"Good lesson. Stayed controlled. Weather changes. Bet it's changed you some too. Watch it more closely next time."

I look out. Across the hillside the storm skids along the ridge, pouring rain as it goes. At least my feet are firmly on the ground. I'm exhausted but thoroughly relieved to have made it to home base, like being breathless after barely outrunning someone in a game of hide-and-seek. But, in this case, the stakes were higher.

"A long time ago I found myself inside an even meaner cloud," Kevin says. "Hail falling so hard I couldn't hear. I thought the airplane would break or somersault."

We get out and tie Bravo's wings down, getting soaked as we pull the ropes tight against the wind.

"Did you call it in as an emergency?"

"I did. And later called it stupidity," he says, "and arrogance. Watch out for those. They get into pilots. It's easy to let happen. Too easy."

I nod.

"Are you alright?"

"Yes. Thanks, Kevin. Good briefing." I look at Bravo, rain dripping from her wingtips. Across the sky a roll of thunder echoes.

"Coming inside?" he asks.

"In a minute."

"Okay. See you."

He hustles across the ramp to the lobby. I lean against Bravo, under her wing, but it gives me no refuge from the rain. The storm's menace softens as the distance between us increases—as only distance can do—and quiets my trembling. But it has left a lasting mark.

The past hour I was in the company of a great evaluator: weather. It leaves its marks on mountains, eroding exposed edges, and whips the seas to redefine shorelines. Like all lands and waters it crosses, it has also left its mark on me.

Beneath my false confidence, now uncovered, is the truth: I could have avoided this monster. Before today I have never known or appreciated such power. Another gust of wind and the tethered wings of my airplane pull against it, leaving them to rock back and forth. Wind and rain and many other things can come along to dissolve our dreams. But not as much as too much ego can.

That night at home, I step softly up the stairs to see my children, undisturbed, in their own worlds. Unannounced and unseen I watch: Annie has lined up her horses, now free from their tiny corrals, and placed them among various toy dogs, bears, and rabbits. The disproportionate sizes of her menagerie are what makes childhood imagination so wonderful. A proud and serious black stallion stares ahead, trying not to notice the large and happy floppy-eared, plush bunny placed next to it. A big, brown bear falls slowly forward on top of the stable, smashing it.

"What have you done now?" says Annie. She assesses the situation, fixes the damage, then murmurs how the dogs need medical treatment. Lucky for them, their able veterinarian comes to their aid. Following fast examinations and positive prognoses, she says, "You will feel fine soon."

I turn to look into Blake's room. His head is down to review a book of science. Then, with eyes closed, recites something from memory, perhaps to last until a test or maybe to last forever. But of this I am certain: He will one day do more than explode his parent's garage. I tiptoe away from eavesdropping on their dreams in the making.

"Mom!" calls Annie when she sees me. "Did you hear the thunder today? We did at school. It was so scary!"

"Yes," I say. "I heard it. It was *very* scary."

The airplane that at first was not airplane enough is now a part of me. I close the door that squeaks, the red interior greeting me with its fragrance of fuel, leather, and chocolate. Today I am solo.

Bravo and I line up at the end of the runway like a runner at the line, waiting for the tower to announce our start. Cleared to begin, I feed Bravo a steady throttle. Momentum mounts, and I can sense it—the very instant when the airplane calls out that the wings are ready. I pull back on the stick. We rise with the wind over the wings and blowing across my face.

My mind is set free from anything else than that of my airplane. Bravo and I join the clear, bright morning air. The freshness is like biting into a crisp, fresh-picked apple. There is nothing else that matters, but I am ready—for almost anything.

So far, all is very standard. In seconds, the hangars below shrink to toy size. *As long as I live, I will never get tired of this.* The morning opens like a prayer.

With final exams only days away, I plan to practice touch-and-go landings into the mild crosswinds. Now united with the sky community, I add my voice to the fast-flowing rhythm of the chorus, each saying what we see and what we will do in a few words: pilot to tower, then back to pilot, pilot to pilot. All the while Bravo's propeller pulses in low timbre.

The downwind leg to the runway is about a mile. Now at 1,000 feet above the ground, I am within minutes of landing. Voices suddenly go silent. Only the humming of the propeller is heard.

I look down off my left shoulder. "Wow! Look at *that*." Below me, following Bravo's shadow on the ground, is a halo ring called a "glory." Glories are early-day phenomena when light, moisture, and temperature are just right. A rainbow ring is encircling my airplane's silhouette as we fly, a present intended just for us.

I have felt flight express beauty in different ways—in sunlit hillsides, in chasing circles of air, in the open arms of waiting runways before me—but none as enchanting as this. At this moment Bravo and I are together inside a glory while suspended in midair. *Breathe.*

Above us, beyond the blue, is the canopy of black eternity that casts its invisible stardust on my wings. Below, a small planet changes seasons in an effort to remind us of time's passage. The dream of wings and ever-faster speed through life has brought me here to this extraordinary moment, between earth and sky, to let me dwell inside this glory. It is truly heaven up here.

In the flash of a few seconds, between takeoff and before rejoining the bonds of Earth, Bravo has shown me infinity—what it takes to be a pilot and what it means to fly. And to not *live small.*

Tower: "83Bravo. Cleared to land. You're number one."

"Number one," I say to Bravo. "That's you!"

"So when do you go before the flying board or whatever it's called?" asks Joan, sitting behind her steaming latte at the coffee shop with the mountains painted on the wall. She's sporting a blue blazer and pencil skirt and pumps.

"In a couple of days. But first," I say, taking a look at her from top to bottom, "don't *you* look professional!"

"My new business look."

"Roger must be so …"

"Roger isn't speaking to me. But no matter. I have plenty to keep me busy. Mike asked me to help him expand his pastry business."

"Well, isn't Roger getting his just desserts in the end!" Helen laughs.

"I owe it to you," Joan says to her.

"Nah. Just worked out well."

"And MJ, you started the Chicks in Charge."

"Well, but you …"

"God forbid either of you should accept some gratitude," she teases.

"We've changed a lot," I say. I can't bring myself to look at Helen, who isn't exactly living a dream.

"So," says Helen, "are you and Mike *business* partners? Or is there more to it?"

"Maybe business. Okay, maybe more. But I have to see where things go. With the bakery. And with Paul."

"*Ohhh* … Paaaaul!" Helen and I say together.

"Things are a bit complicated right now," she says. "But then, they always were. Especially with Roger."

"Well," says Helen, "let us know."

"Will do." Joan takes out a box that says, "Chicks' Buns." "MJ, would you mind taking these to the airfield for me? Maybe drum up some business?"

"Glad to. I'll be there tomorrow. For my exam." I say, battling nerves.

"We've put together something to send you off. Or rather up. Tokens to bring good luck on your exams," Helen says with a gleam in her eye.

Joan hands me a wrapped package. "After your stories about turbulence, I thought you might find these helpful. But hopefully won't need them during the exam."

I remove the wrapping. "Barf bags! Very thoughtful, Joan."

"Use them in good health."

"This is from me," Helen says, handing me a soft package.

I open it. "Helen!" I say with tears coming. "It's perfect!" I put the white scarf around my neck. "They wore these in open-cockpit planes to wipe the oil off their goggles," I explain. "I'll use it for my eyes."

"I'll also light a candle for you too, on your test day," says Joan. "And there's this." I open the last package and pull out a little gold medal with a man raising his arms. "We think St. Joseph is the patron saint of flying,"

179

Joan explains. "He was known for having episodes of levitation anyway. That is, without an airplane. Probably a little nuts."

"I recall being called that too," I say, winking at her.

Joan shakes her head. "Not anymore."

"I'm glad he'll watch over me," I say. "Or maybe beam me up." I look at them, my remarkable friends. Over the past year and a half, we have reached outside of our comfort zones, stretched, hurt, messed up, and kept going. "I will take a little bit of both of you up with me on test day."

"But you can leave this on the ground." Helen hands me one more package.

I open it, and it's the bird's nest photo elegantly framed. "Helen," I sigh, "thank you. I hope I don't disappoint you and be the fledgling that doesn't pass."

"Oh, you'll pass alright. Like all the tests before it—the cards blowing away from you, the radios going silent, the fog, the thunderhead. You'll pass. But not just because of those. Because of all the glories you've seen. You show it. I can see it in your eyes."

The Test

THE FORECAST CAN'T BE RIGHT, so I continue tapping on my computer keys at the kitchen table to recheck aviation weather for the next day: the day of my test. *Refresh data—update. Same thing.*

I pick up my toy airplane. "They have *got* to be kidding. There's no way I'm going up in that."

Already the sky is gray. Not a hazy thin, fog gray but a brooding, dark-mood gray. *Refresh data.* If it's true, then during the morning, when I'm sitting for two or three hours and trying to pass the oral part of the exam, a steady breeze will ride in. After that, when the flying part begins, forecasts will show a change to sustained winds with gusts that could rip the feathers off a starling—or flaps from Bravo. But the forecasts are already hours old. A direct call to aviation weather services could say that things are improving. I dial the number for pilot services.

Weather Briefer: "In your area tomorrow at that time: wind, 25 knots at 3,000. At 4,000, lowering ceiling, gusts at 40."

MJ: "Wind shear. With clouds lowering?"

Weather Briefer: "Yes, ma'am. Do you want to file a flight plan?"

MJ: "I'm a student pilot. My flying exams for my first license are tomorrow." *Silence.* "I guess what I'll do is wait to see what it looks like tomorrow. It might change."

Briefer: "It might."

MJ: "Do you think it will?"

Briefer: "No."

The examiner's office is along the airfield, across from the control tower. He's been at his job a long time, taking pilots of all levels in the air to see how they can manage airplanes of all types. Many commercial airline pilots today have received their flight licenses from him. He is well respected with a you-pass-if-you-earn-it reputation. The latest is that he failed a pilot this week who was seeking an advanced license.

Buffeted by the powerful wind, I have to make two trips to the car to carry all my books and supplies inside: flight bag filled with charts, plans, official test score from my written test, logbook and all the endorsements that say I can take the exams, Bravo's maintenance records to show she is in good shape to fly, my aviation medical card to show I am in good shape to fly, other books in case I am allowed to look up a detail. The white scarf, barf bags, and Flaps are tucked in the bottom and out of sight.

I sit in the waiting room and begin polishing the knees of my jeans. I look at my watch. *He's a few minutes late.* Then five. *I hope Joan is lighting a candle now.* Ten. *Did he cancel due to weather?*

I look out the window and see him. But he's not hurrying inside. He's talking to … *Oh, no, he's talking to Captain Lee!* My stomach flops over a few times. *What if Captain Lee is telling him I'm not ready?* I look away. It's too overwhelming to think about right now. *But what if …*

The door bursts open. "MJ!" he calls out. He's looking at a clipboard, flipping through pages.

"Mr. Kennedy." I jump up, and he shakes my hand. "Nice to …"

"It's Gary. Sorry I'm late. I hate lateness," he says, perturbed, as he unlocks his office door. "Come on in." He takes one step inside. "*Damn!* It's a mess, as usual. I hate that too."

Heart pounding, I begin transferring all my stuff into his office—again, two trips. While Gary, seated at his wide, mahogany desk, waits I desperately start looking for surface space. Some stuff goes on the floor; on a corner of his desk I put materials in the order in which he'll request them as he fills out a form on my candidacy. Finally settled, I take a seat in the leather chair across from him. *Wonder when the last time was that I took a full breath.*

"What the hell is all this?"

"I thought I might need to refer to something," I manage to say. "If it's okay to do that ... in case I don't know something."

"In case you don't *know* something?" he repeats gruffly. "Okay. Let's see what you've got then. Hand me your text."

I pick it up from the floor and push it across the desk. He flips through it. "You've highlighted almost everything."

"Well, in the early months. When I was brand new."

"You don't need all this stuff. Put it back on the floor. Take out a clean sheet of paper. You have one of those, right? Not highlighted?"

"Yes, of course."

I pull out my binder, thick with subject tabs and notes and homework, and take out a sheet of paper. Put the binder back on the floor. Shoot a quick glance out the window—still looks foreboding—and notice that the office brims with everything aviation. The walls are lined with books, manuals, and certificates, noting his awards and achievements. Model airplanes are suspended from the ceiling and float peacefully through the airspace above our heads. A window, with shades half drawn, frames the runways that have become my second home.

Folding his hands over his wide waistline, he says, "Let's begin. Tell me why you're here."

"You mean, why I'm here to take the exams today or ...?"

"I mean, why the license? What made you learn all this?" he asks, gesturing at my aviation library.

"It's what I always wanted. I always knew I would love it. And I do."

"But you could have just learned to fly. Have some enjoyable flights to satisfy you. Or have a few scares and call it a day."

"I thought about it. It's a lot more work than I expected. At least it was for me. Aviation is wonderful, but there's lot to it, and it's hard ..."

"I know," he says, putting up a hand to stop me. "I know how hard it is. Takes gumption."

"I suppose it takes—that," I say. I haven't heard that word in a long time. "Flying surprised me."

"How?"

"Well, it was more than this charming little dream I'd had. It wasn't just the fear and the hard … it was other people's reactions to it. To me. It's been a process, not just learning how to fly but learning how to … live. With the risks. But not letting the risks outweigh the magnificent parts."

"As I say," he responds with what I think is a flicker of a grin, "gumption."

"Gumption," I nod and confirm.

"Give me your aircraft's operating handbook."

I retrieve it from the top of the pile. He thumbs through it, noting all the highlighted passages. I want to explain the categories—pink for limitations, blue for systems, and so on—but somehow keep my mouth shut. Bravo's flight manual is dog-eared from carrying it everywhere.

I'm hoping he won't notice the autographs on the front page. I had the manual with me on a trip to Disneyland. While Jim and the kids were on some kind of ride, I was studying. Chip and Dale, the chipmunks, came over to say hello.

I greeted them politely, and when Dale (or maybe it was Chip) reached for the book to see what I was reading, he spread his arms like airplane wings, as if to say, "Like this!" And then he and Chip (or Dale) opened it and autographed it with a suitably cartoonish flourish.

Sure enough, Gary says, "Chip and Dale *signed* this?"

"Yes." *Explain? Sigh. No.*

"Let's move on," he says, impatiently. Finally I'm up at bat for spring training. His questions are pitched fast and slow. I get most of them. He gives me some time to rethink others and give a better reply.

He looks over my FAA written exam and the few questions missed. "What? How could *any*one miss the definition of *nighttime*? Of all the questions to miss!"

"Well, I mixed up the three *night times:* one for lights on, when to log night flight, what time does civilian nightfall start … I should have slowed down and reread it," I confess.

He hands me some aviation weather reports and asks what I can interpret from a forecast that's buried in the middle. I answer his question on the airspace limits in the areas he points to, what they're called, and when I can fly in them. The navigation charts come next, and I think of Tom and the morning we studied together so long ago.

Almost two hours later he says, "Now, on your blank page, do some calculations on determining air density and takeoff roll. What you would do if you took off at Lake Tahoe on a hot afternoon and why. Diagram the fuel system and pitot-static system from memory. Discuss with me later what happens if your airspeed indicator fails. Tell me what the fuel reserves are for a night flight ..." and he lists others on a board, including the weight and balance configurations for Bravo. He tells me he weighs 280 pounds—data I need for the calculation. "I'm going to leave you alone for a while. Take your time."

"Is it okay if I take out a snack? While I work on this list?"

"Sure," he says. "Or you can have mine. My wife has me on a diet and packed me an apple. I hate apples." He walks out.

It is late morning, but the office has grown darker. The floating airplanes overhead swing wider and occasionally bump each other. The shade at the window is tapping in double time. I get up to look at the runways. The windsock is straight out and trembling. The weather briefer forecasts were right. *I'm supposed to fly in another two hours, for another two hours.*

The weight and balance numbers are way out of scale because Gary is way off the scale and really should start eating those apples he hates. Bravo will only accommodate him if I take out some weight; the only thing I can remove is fuel. If I put Gary in, take out several gallons, and fly for just two hours, all will be well—if the weather improves.

I call the mechanic at the hangar. "Did you fill Bravo this morning?"

"Of course. But you're not going to fly in *this* weather, are you?"

"I haven't looked at the forecast for a couple of hours." A flash of lightning streaks across the western sky. "But we can't go full. Gary's too big. Take out eight gallons."

The mechanic chuckles. "He told me his wife's got him on a diet. Puts him in a bad mood."

"Just what I need," I say. "Don't forget to take out the fuel—in case the weather lets me fly."

When Gary returns, he looks as grim as the weather outside. "Okay? All done?"

"Yes."

He takes my pages and murmurs through the answers. "Yeah, good, good. Yeah, close enough ... *wait*. This one here though. Tahoe. You should always circle on that one—the air density is too low at that temperature and pressure. Be sure to do that when you go there!" He continues to review the answers. "Good work. Nice diagrams. Yeah, okay, okay ... okay." He looks up. "Better than most. Passed the oral and calculations." He balls up my paper and tosses it into a full trash bin.

"Really? Yes? *Yes*. Thank you. Thank you!" I let out a breath and slump down in my seat. The wind piccolos through the window and quiets down again. "What, I wonder," I muse aloud, "do other mothers do on a Saturday morning?"

Gary has begun the FAA paperwork and is looking over my logbook. He stops. I sit up, knowing I misspoke. He slaps his hands down on his desk. *I blew it.* "I think it's ..." He starts to bellow.

"I mean, what I meant is," I stammer, "there are other ways to spend a morning." *Shut up!*

"It's marvelous! Nothing good comes easy. *Nothing!* You see these airplanes above you?" When I nod, he goes on. "Flown every one of them. Decades of flying. A lifetime of flying. One of the dearest joys of my life. Other than my kids, of course. Let me tell you about a flight just last summer ..." And off he goes, stepping into a realm of magical reminiscing: back in time, back to each airplane, how it felt and what he saw. I feel it. I see it too. When he comes back to Earth again, he seems startled to see me there. He clears his throat.

"Gary," I say, "would you like to try something a friend of mine made?" I pull out and unwrap one of Joan's Chicks' Buns.

Gary's eyes brighten. "Oh, God, sure. Just don't tell my wife." He takes a bite and rolls his eyes. "Mmm! Kicks the crap outa that apple. You said your *friend* makes them? Does she sell them too?"

"She's just started a new bakery business with a partner. I'll tell her to make the airfield one of her stops."

He looks at me. "You know," he says, pointing, "you could be a poster pilot."

"A poster pilot? Like an if-she-can-do-it-you-can-too kind of poster pilot?"

"No, no. Nothing like that. A you-should-get-off-your-ass-and-do-something-too kind of poster."

I smile, flattered. Just then, thunder rolls.

"Gary, what does the radar on your screen show? Any red?"

"Let's see." He snaps on his computer to show radar screens for precipitation and a moving storm. "It's overhead now. Think it will pass in a little while?"

I look at the screen and back to the window to see the real thing. The clouds are heavy and bulbous. Then go back to see the picture of a long, curved line—a cold front, with blue, triangle-shaped plates along it, like the back of a dragon. *Not again. One experience is enough.*

"What do you think?" he presses. "We'd have to cancel the test. The FAA office hates when tests are discontinued—extra paperwork."

"Microbursts," I say, referring to the sudden downdrafts that come with a cold front like this.

"What about them?"

"They tear you up in seconds after takeoff. I have to reschedule." I'm devastated.

He stares at me and begins to swivel in his seat again. "Reschedule?"

"Yes. I can't fly today."

He stands. "Good call. That's it. *Gumption.* I love gumption. I'll let the FAA know we'll take it from here. Tomorrow. Let's resume, only with the flying test first thing. Hey, um, before you go … got any more of those buns?"

The next morning the world is calm, except for my heart that's back to racing. All is memorized—all the maneuvers. No cards go along with me; just my headset, charts, checklists, and kneepad to jot down short notes from the tower. With Bravo light on fuel and heavy with examiner, we take off. Gary gives me his orders: Go out to the practice area, he'll pick the road, and I will perform an S-turn along that line. I set it up.

"Beginning the maneuver," I say. "Winds from behind, I roll to the left and into the wind, cross the line, and immediately roll right …" to tell him what I'm thinking and doing.

He grunts a few times.

"Completing S-turn …" and roll out. "Good?"

"Might be a fluke. Keep going." As I swing back and forth above a country road, he says, "Pretty good. Enough of those. No fluke, I guess." Then he says to climb higher and go into tight, steep turns, right, then left. "Show me that left one again. You can do a better rollout than that."

I'm grateful to have a second chance, and this time we get a bump from Bravo's wake.

"Okay, better. That's how." He scribbles more notes. "Divert to Napa County airport."

I bring out my charts to estimate the distance and headings. As we're nearing Napa, I call up the airfield information, and they clear me to land. Yellow mustard flowers carpet hillsides on the vineyards below.

Close to the runways, Gary pulls the power out. "You just lost all power. What do you do?"

I set up to land directly to the numbers at the end of the runway, watching my glide speed.

"Lucky you—your power came back," he says. "You can land with power." Then, "Oh, look. Buffalo on the field. Go around!"

I do it. The test "emergencies" are unnerving, but I stay focused. Sweating and sticking to the seat but focused. On our way back to the northern end of the delta, I ask him what his most frightening emergency has ever been.

"You don't want to know right now," he moans. "Okay. My oil blew all over the windscreen. Had to land in the field and couldn't see outside, so …"

Right. Didn't really want to know right now.

At no time does Gary scream, hyperventilate, or announce, "My airplane!" after my demonstrations, which would be a way to tell me that

188

I've failed. At least not yet. He calls up Concord to tell them that Bravo will be making multiple approaches.

His familiar voice is quickly acknowledged by the tower, who adds several "yes, sirs" into their replies after every request he makes. When Gary's in the sky, everyone sweats.

Almost two hours later, after I've executed almost all the maneuvers on the list, he tells me to taxi off the runway. Relieved, I'm still not sure of his decision. He continues to scribble. I change the frequency to talk to ground control and am happy when I recognize Martin's voice. Martin, like the rest of the tower, knows it's me and that the examiner is sitting to my right.

Ground: "83Bravo, take Alpha to Charlie and over to the ramp."

MJ: "Alpha, Charlie to ramp. 83Bravo. Thanks."

"Just a second. Before you taxi," says Gary. Bravo and I wait for what seems a very long time. Gary looks like he's tallying something, then drops his pen to his lap. "Let's go inside and finish the paperwork."

"How did I do?" I ask, finally looking over at him.

"I said, 'Let's finish the paperwork,' not rip it up. You passed."

"I *did*? I passed?" Unsure if I heard it right, I repeat, "I passed? That's great! Thank you." I feel exhausted.

"If you don't mind my asking, MJ, why are you so surprised?"

I hesitate. *Should I ...? Yes.* "I saw you talking to Captain Lee before my written exam yesterday. And, well ... he and I didn't exactly see eye to eye sometimes. Well, *ever*. And I was afraid that he'd say something about me."

"Actually," Gary says, "he did."

I feel sick. *How dare he ...*

"He said that you were one of the most dedicated pilots he'd ever had."

I'm too surprised to answer right away, but finally I find my voice. "Thank you," I say again and squeeze my grip on the controls, making Bravo's wings rock a little.

"You're welcome," Gary says. Then he laughs. "*Hummer.*"

At home that night, after hours of hugs and hoorays, I am back to my old routine. After what I will hold dear for the rest of my life, laundry and squabbling children and dinners waiting to be scorched wait for me. The usual basics of home life. Absently folding, I think of Bravo on the ramp, now under a star-filled sky.

"Mom?" asks Annie at the doorway, hiding an oversized paper behind her. She pulls it around and shows it to me. "It took me a while," she says, beaming, "but I know it took you even longer." On it is a universe of dots and a carefully hand-drawn line connecting one to the next. "D'you like it?"

I kneel down to try to decipher it. "Of course. Of course, I do." I don't know what it is and don't dare guess.

"It's what you said you'd have to do. And you *did* it."

"I did it. But, wh …"

"A thousand dots. Remember? You connected all of them. Like you said you'd have to do."

The paper drops to the floor, and Annie puts her arms around me.

"So what's next?"

"Probably the next license. There's so much more to learn."

"We sort of thought that might happen," says Joan, "so we got you something."

She hands me a small package. I open it: highlighters! While we're laughing, Mike bursts through the door.

"I thought I might find you Chicks here!" he says, panting happily. "I need you, Joan. Back at the shop. Quick. Orders are going crazy." To our surprise and delight, he kisses her.

"Duty calls!" She grabs her briefcase and says to us, "Sorry, have to go."

"Good-bye," we say.

After they've left, Helen adds, "And good-bye, Roger. He moved out. Did she tell you?"

"No!"

"She's rewriting her old rule book."

"I'm proud of her."

"Me too."

"So, Helen … what are you up to today?"

"I'm leading some groups on how to survive what you don't plan for."

I sit back and stare in admiration. "I guess you're a bit of an expert on that."

"I guess I am. You know, MJ, while I was getting treatment I kept running into other cancer patients, and the ones who were almost done all said the same thing: Once you survive cancer, you're a different person. You're stronger, and the little things that used to drive you crazy don't even bother you anymore. So many of them said they were grateful. Imagine? Grateful for having had cancer! But I'll tell you something. Once I finished, I got it. Cancer was my dragon, and I slayed him. That feels amazing."

Will told me that when I got my license I could fly to a small café—a pilot favorite called Jonesy's, located along an airfield in the wine country. I had promised Blake he would be my first officer of that flight.

"Ready? You take the controls, Blake."

He nods, his headset covering a lot more than his ears. He peers out over the panel looking west, but Bravo is turning east, toward the hills.

"Steer it more this way," I say, taking my side of the stick to correct our course. Now Blake takes over, but we're going too far west. A few bumps of wind and Bravo bounces.

"Take it! Take it back, Mom!" shouts Blake.

We land at the airfield, tucking Bravo alongside the other small aircraft. Blake helps me tie down the airplane and gallops inside.

We're greeted at once by a waitress who leads us to a table, and then hands us menus. She's wearing a short, black dress and white apron, and graying hair is pinned neatly under a black bonnet scalloped in white, just like the pictures of the uniforms on the walls of the early days when this café opened.

"I'll give you a minute," she says. After taking stock of us for moment, adds, "You fly in—together?"

"Yes. First flight together," I smile. "New pilot."

"Good," she sighs, "for you. Wish I could do something new. Been here too long."

"I'm all set," Blake says, having already scanned the menu. "I'd like a cheeseburger with sautéed mushrooms and extra French fries, please."

"I'll have a salad, thanks," I say, handing the menus back. "And two milks."

She says she'll be right back and retreats. I look out the windows to the airfield. The windsock is swinging gently. As usual, the westerlies are picking up. Lots of greasy food, small and bouncy airplane. Then I remember: I have Joan's gift of motion-sickness bags. The generous portions soon arrive.

Blake stares at the bounty of fries and mushrooms but looks unhappy. *Something's wrong.*

"Mom," he begins, "I've been thinking about telling you that I want you to know how glad I am, really happy, that you like flying airplanes. Please don't be upset," he says.

"What is it, Blake? What's the matter?"

"I—I just don't like them," he confesses, holding me captive with soft eyes. "I'm glad that you do. But I don't like airplanes."

Disappointment sweeps through me. Of all the family, he was the one I most expected to love the skies the most, like me. He understood, the night of the storm, about how flight feels for me and how we planned on this first flight together.

But have to swallow it and manage to say, as convincingly as I can, "Blake, of *course* I don't mind."

"You sure?"

"I'm sure." But I'm not. "You don't have to like it because I do. Go ahead. Enjoy your lunch," I say and toast his milk glass with mine.

I glance out at Bravo. I look at the airplane but see how much happier Blake seems now that he has told me his dark secret. Outside is only a small airplane. Across the table is my child, of my heart and soul, who has so tenderly acknowledged, encouraged even, my passion but asked for my forgiveness for not loving it too. Where is my allegiance? Blake or Bravo? My son or an airplane? The choice is clear. This cannot divide us. I cannot be both a mother and a pilot.

My heart sinks. I cannot bear to see him sad. How did I not know this before? I look outside again, unable to reconcile it. A simple fix rushes in: *This is my farewell to you, Bravo.*

For the rest of the meal, I listen to his excitement about his latest science projects and the rocket propulsion system he's going to be working on over the summer. I nod when he wants to order more sautéed mushrooms. *What difference will it make? After all, it's the final flight for us both.*

Out on the ramp, I think of all the times I approached Bravo with anticipation. *Not now. Not ever again.* We prepare Bravo as usual and taxi to the end of the runway for takeoff.

Tower: "Cleared for takeoff, 83Bravo. Good flight."

MJ: "Cleared for takeoff. 83Bravo. Good-bye, Tower."

But then it happens. The magic that began so many months ago returns, as it always did, as it's doing now. My airplane stretches out to the horizon as we return to the skies. I am not separate from the wings. Flying has given me a glory that I cannot change.

"Wow, look at the hills!" says Blake. I give my mushroom-filled passenger other things to look at on the horizon: bay bridges, cargo ships, and a bird sanctuary the examiner had me circle—all to help take his mind off bumpy Bravo.

"Over there," I point below, "is where you and Annie and Dad and I watched the camel races one summer." We both start to laugh, recalling how one spit on Annie.

I call in to land. But I'm a few hundred feet too high coming down on the final approach to the runway.

"Blake."

"What?" he says, looking out, his eyes wide. "Is everything okay?"

"Yes, fine. I need to lose a little altitude."

"On *purpose?*"

"Of course. This is how it's done."

"How," he asks meekly, "is it done? Tell me when it's done."

I slip Bravo into a sideways, wing-down, graceful descent. But it does look wrong when the passenger knows the runway has a different heading.

"Mom! Where are we *going?* Ah!"

193

"It's okay! It's done." *Done quite well too.*

I realign the nose. We are almost over the numbers, then above the numbers, and then power is out. Bravo loses momentum. We float a short distance on the warm air, slowing. *Squeak.*

I love this so much.

My heart soars. I can choose to love them both.

Epilogue

"THIS?" ASKS THE NEW flight student, who is surveying the modest proportions of the aircraft she has just been introduced to. "But it's ... so *small.*"

I look at it too, as a new flight instructor, this needing-a-new-coat-of-wax airplane with the faded red stripe. After six years and several hundred hours of flying time, I took more flight tests and earned several more licenses. But the other lessons were even more vital and were tested too: how fear misleads, how truth is hard won, and how, if I had not taken the risk to try a dream, I would never be living the life today that I once imagined years ago. The pilot licenses I hold are not just about knowing how to fly an airplane but how I've rewritten my life's story and feel there is a new destiny still in store for me.

I want to tell my student how I faced ravenous dragons that over time were tamed, minute by minute, until one morning the glory of flight was mine. Bravo is a very small airplane that can transport you to the sky and show you your soul. But she needs to come to that on her own. Like I did.

Instead, I ask, "Shall we get inside and see what can happen in this small airplane?"

She hesitates, looking doubtful. "I've always wanted to try."

When we open the doors, the scents of fuel, chocolate, and leather greet us. I smile and reach into my tan jacket for a peppermint.

The checklists are complete. We begin our journey to find our dream.

"Clear!" I yell out my side window.

Bravo roars to life.

Acknowledgements

WHEN YOU BEGIN a dream and take the first step up to new skies, you may not yet be aware that your journey will be life changing or include numerous others who will be instrumental in giving you the critical lift to make it happen. But, when you find your wow, may you also find these people who will be there for you too, and thank them with all your heart.

For helping you see the world in a new way, you will want to salute each of your instructors for teaching you, for their courage to let you make mistakes and to discover not just how to be a pilot but what it means to be flying. They will make what looks so improbable a wondrous reality.

Be sure to find and give special thanks to friends who listen and give insights, and advisors who critique and cheer for you. All of them—and you—will find out that writing a book about a dream is even harder than doing the actual dream. May you have a team like the Chicks in Charge, as well as Tammie, Mary Jane, Robin, John, Marion, Sandra, Denisa, Gail, Pascale, all the Net Wits, Ken, Lynne, and Russ. To so many others too, my sincere gratitude for your good wishes along the way.

May you meet an author like Linda McFarland, an angel, who will introduce you to Randy Peyser of Author One Stop, who will find a publisher for your story. Mine was fortunate enough to land at Big Table Publishing. May you work with someone as wonderful as Robin Stratton, an editor with endless patience. She is the kind of copilot you want next to you when charting a course, beginning with "Once upon a time ..." all the way through until "The End." It was a journey of many miles in between, but one that I am so very grateful to have taken with Robin by my side. I am deeply thankful for Joanne Shwed, my copyeditor and interior designer, who spotted everything and added a fabulous finishing touch.

Finally, may you have, as I am blessed to have, a family who continues to love you when you fall in love with doing what you always wanted to do, who encourages you to write your story about it, and even lets you include them in the telling of it. May you also have the most loving partner and best friend, as I do in my husband Jim, who will believe in you and want you to grow. Every pilot should be so fortunate.

To you, dear reader, may this book help you begin your own takeoff, so that you also do what makes your heart fly higher. Begin it now. Don't let fear rule your life. At any age, it's never too late to follow your dream. Being a pilot is an experience that has given me profound joy and deep, personal satisfaction. I wish for you the same feeling when you experience your own wow.

MJM
May 2016
Lafayette, California

Six Lessons on How to Embrace Your Dreams Now

What a pilot learned from the sky

SIGN UP FOR THIS FREE GUIDE

mjmarggraff.com/free-guide

I welcome your remarks, will read them, and will personally reply as quickly as possible. I've found great joy in flying and hope that this book will inspire and motivate you to follow your dream. It will change your life. Please contact me at www.mjmarggraff.com.

CPSIA information can be obtained
at www.ICGtesting.com
Printed in the USA
BVOW03s0157250917

495799BV00001B/5/P